The Feathers of My Wings

By Jerome Lee John II

Copyright © Jerome Lee John II

Copyright/Disclaimer

Copyright © 2019 Jerome Lee John II - All rights reserved. This book or parts thereof may not be reproduced in any form, stored in any retrieval system, or transmitted in any form by any means—electronic, mechanical, photocopy, recording, or otherwise—without prior written permission of the publisher, except as provided by United States of America copyright law. For permission requests, contact the author or publisher.

ISBN: 9781798488072
ISBN: 9780578467573

Dedication

To my momma and daddy, Ravonda and Jerome John. For constantly teaching and building me to become a good young man. Even though at times it was hard. To my Sister, Amanda for always being the guiding light, protection and telling me things sooner so I could avoid them later.

To my niece, Payshence Aryanna John. By the time you are old enough to read this book it will be in your toy chest collecting dust. You will have gotten older and with your own personal experiences that will have groomed you to fly even farther than I. May this book help give you power, wisdom and knowledge beyond measure.

Epigraph

Don't Quit
By: Edgar Albert Guest

When things go wrong, as they sometimes will, when the road you're trudging seems all uphill when the funds are low and the debts are high, and you want to smile but you have to sigh, when care is pressing you down a bit rest if you must, but don't you quit. Life is queer with its twists and turns.

As everyone of us sometimes learns. And many a fellow turns about when he might have won had he stuck it out. Don't give up though the pace seems slow you may succeed with another blow. Often the goal is nearer than it seems to a faint and faltering man;

Often the struggler has given up when he might have captured the victor's cup; and he learned too late when the night came down, how close he was to the golden crown. Success is failure turned inside out - the silver tint of the clouds of doubt, and when you never can tell how close you are, it may be near when it seems afar; so stick to the fight when you're hardest hit it's when things seem worst, you must not quit.

By: Edgar Albert Guest

Acknowledgements

Thanks to everyone that has contributed to this book and it's creation. It has truly been a labor of love, and your support means a lot to me. Thank you for picking a copy of this project. If you find this book thought provoking or useful to yourself or anyone be sure to share it with a loved one.

Contents

The Feathers of My Wings 2
Dedication 4
Epigraph 5
Acknowledgements 7
Introduction 9
PART ONE 10
CHAPTER 1 NO GRAY 11
CHAPTER 2 LOOK DOWN! 21
CHAPTER 3 WALKING THE PAST 34
CHAPTER 4 USE YOUR HANDS 41
CHAPTER 5 THOMAS EDISON 49
PART TWO 57
CHAPTER 6 I AM DYING 58
CHAPTER 7 WALK WITH A LIMP 70
CHAPTER 8 DAMMIT I FELL 81
CHAPTER 9 MEND WHAT IS BROKEN 90
CHAPTER 10 FROM SCRATCH 96
PART THREE 106
CHAPTER 11 SMILE, SCHOLASTIC SCHOLAR 107
CHAPTER 12 FIND YOUR VOICE 125
CHAPTER 13 MENS ET MANUS 141
CHAPTER 14 STRETCH YOUR WINGS 151

Introduction

I wrote this book in the hopes that you will read it and become inspired. The name of the book is called 'The Feathers of My Wings'. This is a memoir about a few key events that have taken place in my life that have shaped me to become the young man that I am. I named this book 'The Feathers of My Wings' based on the idea that we all have bad experiences and good ones. These experiences are the feathers that God allows in our lives to mold us, develop our strengths and endurance to help us fly and reach our goals. While reading this story you will journey through the experiences, emotions and most importantly the lessons that I learned along the way. My goal is that you can use the lessons I learned as a tool that can be applied to your life.

PART ONE

CHAPTER 1
NO GRAY

There would be an intimidating car ride after school that day. It all started when a girl started picking on me during recess. I don't even remember why I was being picked on. It was one of those childish moments when someone says you have the cooties and then you all start arguing.

When recess was over we had to line up to go back inside. While the girl and I were arguing back and forth in line, she spit in my face. I started to feel anger and a level of confusion that I had never experienced before. When she walked away, I held in all the anger, sadness, and confusion.

Once we got inside, I realized there would be a brief moment where I would walk past her. I saw my opportunity and wanted to take it.

Just when I was about to pass her, I tapped on her shoulder, gathered all the liquid I could in my mouth, and spit right back in her face. I ran down the hallway to my class feeling relieved that I didn't get caught.

Class was about to start and I felt like I was home free. Suddenly, I saw the girl and a teacher walk through the door. I knew they were looking for me.

I kept my head down hoping I wouldn't be noticed and they would overlook me. When I lifted my head up to see if they had gone and moved on, I heard a shout.

"There he is!"

She called me out and the teacher told me to come with her and leave the class. In that moment, I felt like my life was over. They were going to tell my parents and I was going to get a beating like all the other times when I got into trouble.

I was scared of my parents, but more scared of my daddy than my momma. My momma was nice to me. She treated me well, and at worst I would get a slap on the hand and be scolded. My daddy on the other hand—it took the breath out of me to describe the type fear I felt when they mentioned his name.

I walked out into the hallway, already knowing what this was going to be about. I decided I would tell the truth.

"Jerome did you spit in her face?" the teacher asked.

"No, I did not spit in that girl's face." I lied about everything; all the courage in me dropped the moment the heat was on. We went back and forth; back and forth—both lying about what the other had done.

"Jerome, I'm going to call your parents."

The worst was happening.

"No, no, no, please don't call them! Call anybody else but them!" I pleaded.

I wanted to get down on both knees and beg for another chance. The teacher grabbed my hand and started guiding me down the hall to the principal's office. The hallway seemed to be stretching longer and longer as the tears rolled down my face.

I snatched my hand away from the teacher and tried to make a run for it. I knew this was my only chance to get away. But just as I broke away, she grabbed me again. I kept resisting and pulling away.

I knew that if I was forced to go into the office, it would be all over for me. The teacher finally wrapped her arms around my waist and dragged me to the front office.

We finally got into the front office, the teacher sweating and breathing hard. I continued to cry as I waited for my mother to come.

But it was my daddy that walked through the door. I kept my eyes down. They had already told him what I had done. I felt his anger glaring at me.

"Get up, son, let's go."

"Sir, you have to sign him out."

"I do not need permission to take my son from anywhere. I am not signing my son out of school when you called me to come get him from school," my daddy responded.

"But, sir."

"No. I am not going to say it again. Did I sign him in when I dropped him off? Then I am not signing him out."

He turned around and walked out.

"Come on."

To make sure I stayed safe as long as possible, I walked ten steps behind him. I didn't want to be within striking distance. I felt as if everything important to me would vanish in the blink of an eye if I got closer than ten steps.

He stopped and snapped his fingers.

"Speed up. Walk with me."

This was it. We made our way to the car and got in. He started asking me questions like:

"Son, what happened?

You think it's okay to spit in a person's face?

Why did you do that?

What did she do to you?"

To all of these questions I replied with "I don't know." or silence.

At this age, I was not a very confident boy. I didn't know how to express my feelings. I could speak, but when I experienced any type of pressure and was forced to speak, my mind always went blank.

"Okay, son. I don't know what to do. I told you everything I know about how to succeed in school and you still won't do the right thing."

We sat in the car in silence. I tried to prepare myself for the beating that was coming.

My daddy grabbed the gearshift and I jumped. He was grabbing the gearshift slowly and calmly, but his hand could have come up fast. I pressed myself against the door to brace myself for impact. We rode around for about ten to fifteen minutes in silence before he spoke again.

"Jerome, if you fail, I fail. If you have short comings, then I do too. As a father, I am responsible for your wellbeing. It is my job to make sure you are prepared for what the world is going to throw at you.

Right now, you are doing everything wrong and I don't know what else to say to help you. I have told you everything to do to be successful. What else can I say to help you understand that going down this road is not the answer to the problems you face?"

The car was silent for a few moments.

"Tell me something because I have done everything I know to do."

"I don't know, Daddy."

We drove for a few more minutes; it felt strange because nothing was happening the way I expected it to happen and I was starting to feel a little relieved.

While driving, we started going across a bridge. My daddy suddenly stopped the car and pushed the button for his emergency signal. This bridge was above highway 74 and there were a total of four lanes on this highway, and there was no shoulder on the side for you to pull over if your car broke down. My daddy stopped in the middle of the lane on the bridge.

He took his seatbelt off and turned to me.

"Son, I want you to take your seatbelt off, open the door, and get out. Put one of your legs across the fence and hold on to the fence.

Now Jerome, this is the tricky part, because when you let go of that fence, you have to time it in such a way that you hit a car.

You can't pick any car, you have to wait for an eighteen-wheeler, because if you get hit by a regular car, you're going to break a rib or two, probably some limbs, and then you will be in pain before you die.

I love you and I don't want you to be in pain, so I would prefer that you wait for an eighteen-wheeler and get hit by that. Then you will die instantly and there will be no pain."

After he gave me these instructions, I just sat there with my seatbelt off. It was like I was in a daze. I didn't understand the request. I sat there staring at the glove compartment.

"Jerome, open the door and go ahead, son!" my daddy yelled.

He reached across me and opened the door for me.

"Go ahead!"

I sat there silently without moving a muscle.

"Listen son, if you fail, I fail. If you fall short, so do I. If you have any shortcomings, I have them too. If you die, that means I die too. If you jump off this bridge right now, I will follow right behind you. At this point, I can't go home without you, so that means I have to go where you go. Make a decision.

The choice you make will decide your life and mine if we have to die."

"There are only three ways to live this life, and only one of them is the right way. If you lie, cheat, and steal, you will end up in jail for the rest of your life and die there. If you still decide to do all those things, you will end up in the streets where somebody will kill you.

The other option is to choose to do the right thing. Be honest, loyal, respectful, trustworthy, and live a healthy life that will bring nothing but positivity.

Right now, son, you are going down one of the wrong roads, and I'm not going to watch you do it. I want to spare you a life full of pain. You represent me and my teachings—decide whether we are going to live or die. Are you going to think about your choices and make the right decision, or continue to do wrong?"

I slowly looked up and turned my head towards the bridge. I looked back to see my daddy glaring at me.

"No."

"Close the door, son," he replied.

He started the car again and we drove off. What I was used to happening started to take place. I got hit in the head, chest, and legs. It got so bad we almost ran off the road. Finally, he stopped hitting me and said,

"Son, just do the right thing."

This day changed my life forever; that moment is when reality came to face me. I had to start making decisions, and they were going to be hard choices to make. Choices I would have to answer to for the rest of my life. Do we live or die? Are you going to be honest or not? Are you going to be a fair man, a just man, or not? Are you trustworthy or aren't you? Are you going to be the man that does what he says he is going to do? There is only black or white, yes or no. There is NO GRAY! Those questions will always resonate with me. The real question is—after you make your choice, who are you going to affect, and in what way?

CHAPTER 2
LOOK DOWN!

"Jerome, it's time to get up." My momma called. It was time for school. Seven a.m. came quickly. On these mornings, the bathroom was the best time for me to get extra sleep. I would lock the bathroom door, run the sink water, and lay across the floor and go back to sleep. After about another five to ten minutes, I would get up to wash my armpits and brush my teeth, and then head back to my room to get dressed.

I often had the pleasure of talking to my daddy before school in the morning, and those conversations were always very serious. One morning, he spoke to me about how to defend myself. He used to say,

"Son, if someone puts their hands on you and they don't stop when you tell them too, even after you ask them to stop multiple times, then you have my permission to ball your fists up and hit them square in the jaw. And don't you stop hitting them, either."

"Okay, Daddy."

"Now listen, son. This is important. If a white man calls you a nigga, don't say anything at all. I want you to walk away and go find a boulder. Something you can put in your hand, even if it's a rock. It can even be a brick.

You then have my permission, in fact, I command you to hit him on the side of his head as hard as you can. I guarantee you will never be called a nigga by him ever again."

I didn't understand why I was being told all of this, so I just responded and said okay.

My momma took me to school every morning on her way to work. I never did like riding the bus and we only lived about ten minutes away from the school anyway.

South Scotland Elementary was a very interesting school to say the least. There were a lot of thought-provoking things and situations that happened there, and nothing you did could prepare you mentally to face them. This was because of the way they taught at the school, but was also due to the school's location and the teachers that taught there.

My elementary school was a developing school constantly trying to grow and change the atmosphere and learning experience for the students.

South Scotland was not in the middle of the city or in an urban area where kids could walk to school. It was located deep in the country. Everything that surrounded the school was cotton fields and farmland. During the spring, you could see all the cotton fields surrounding the school blossom and turn into cotton balls ready to be harvested. During the spring and summer months, you could look out into the distance and see nothing but white fields of cotton.

When it came to school, I lived for recess. I could run and play kickball if I wanted to, or I could climb through the jungle gym and do as many pull-ups as I possibly could. At one point I even set the school record for doing the most pull-ups. I felt so alive and I loved being outdoors during recess.

When I was eleven years old, everything was a competition, especially during recess, and nothing else mattered except winning and not getting into trouble or getting your feelings hurt. One day at recess, we all got on the swings and tried to see who could go the highest. After we were done swinging, Kevin and I started arguing about who went the highest and who beat who racing down the hill. He knew that I always beat him racing to the bottom of the hill. Today we just decided to start arguing about it, which quickly led to an exchange of insults.

"That's why you ugly," he said.

"You ugly," I responded.

By now there was a crowd of kids around us and everyone was staring at us. The teachers were talking to each other and not paying attention.

"You stupid," he said.

"You stupid," I responded.

"Your momma stupid," he replied.

He started talking about my momma so I said something about his momma.

Suddenly, he got really mad.

"You better stop talking about my momma," he yelled.

I showed a confused expression on my face because he was the one who brought them into the conversation.

I looked at him, walked up closer, and said,

"Ya momma."

He pushed me as hard as he could.

I told him to stop pushing me, but he pushed me again. After he pushed me three times, I was tired and pretty upset.

I balled my fist, leaned back, and punched him in the face. I kept hitting him and he started fight back. He grabbed me, wrapped his arms around my waist, and tried to pick me up and slam me to the ground. I wrapped my arms around him as well to avoid getting picked up. We started pulling and tugging each other trying to slam each other to the ground. I heard my best friend Jamael in the background screaming, "Get him, Jerome, get him!"

Dirt was flying in the air and the other kids gathered around to watch the fight. Nothing like this had ever happened to me before.

Finally, Mrs. Ogletree, my homeroom teacher, ran over and pulled us apart. She grabbed both of us by our collars and pulled us away from one another. Then she began escorting us to the principal's office. As we were walking, Kevin and I tried to get in extra hits by reaching around the back and front of Mrs. Ogletree.

At the principal's office, we had to meet with Ms. Madison. Ms. Madison was a tall, slender lady with grey hair. She always had bags under her eyes and seemed tired all the time. She was my fourth grade teacher and this year she had moved up to become the principal for the entire school. Ms. Madison was a special person to me. She was more interested in me than any of the other students—and not in a good way. She used to point out when I would do something wrong as an example to the other kids because often it was a mistake they were making as well. For example, when I got a problem wrong it was pointed out to the other students that I got it wrong but this is how you do it correctly.

Ms. Madison had Kevin and I come into her office individually to tell her what happened. She then gave us papers to take home and have our parents sign to let them know we got into a fight. If we got the papers signed, we would not get suspended from school. Each day we waited without signed papers would add a day onto our suspension. If the papers were still not signed after three days, we would be suspended for three days and have to do community service.

I didn't know how I was going to tell my momma and daddy I got suspended from school, especially since I had just got in trouble for not turning in homework and disturbing class. I couldn't come home with another bad report. I had to figure out a way to get around it.

For the next few days, I avoided the conversation and didn't say anything about the fight or the suspension. I didn't like getting into trouble because it seemed like I always had to answer questions I didn't know the answer to. I was not good at explaining myself and didn't have a lot of confidence when it came to school or anything that I did.

The third day came and it was an ordinary morning. On the way to school, I had the opportunity to tell my momma. She drove me all the way to school that morning and dropped me off, but I didn't say anything. I got out of the car without a plan or idea for what I was going to do, even though I had been thinking about it all morning.

I went through the entire day and didn't see Ms. Madison until my math class. She interrupted class and told me to come with her. Getting up out my seat, I knew it was all over. I was going to be in trouble. We walked out of class and made it to the principal's office Ms. Madison called my momma and she ended up having to come out to the school and get me.

When my momma arrived, she just stared at me. I knew my momma didn't like coming out to the school for this kind of stuff. She had to leave work and come out to deal with a situation she had taught me not to get into anyway. I knew I should not have fought Kevin. I should have just walked away. But instead I was sitting there again, nervous, and without answers to any of the questions they were asking me.

"Jerome why didn't you just have me sign the permission slip?" my momma asked.

"I didn't want to get into trouble."

"So, you thought that not getting it signed would be the best strategy to not get into trouble?" she asked, "Because now you are in trouble."

"I thought it would buy me some time to figure out how to avoid the situation and not get into trouble," I explained.

That was not a good idea.

"I am not upset you got into a fight. I am upset you didn't want to deal with the consequences of fighting," my momma said.

I didn't have anything to say at this point. My daddy told me how to deal with the fighting situation, but he didn't tell me I would have to go through this even though I did everything he said.

I felt like everyone in the room thought it was dumb and crazy. I was the only one who thought it made sense to not want to be in trouble.

My momma and Ms. Madison arranged that I would do three weeks of community service instead of three days of suspension since my momma and daddy worked during the day.

At the time, I didn't know what community service was. I was just glad I didn't get into too much trouble or get a beating. My daddy was always saying, "Boy, you keep it up and yo ass gon' be grass."

Instead of going to recess on Monday, I reported to the principal's office to start my community service. At the principal's office, Ms. Madison handed me latex gloves, a container of trash bags, and an orange vest.

I then followed her outside to the front of the school where she told me to get in the ditch by the front of the school. She stood at the top of the hill and told me to put the vest on.

"Now, I want you to pick up all the pinecones and put them in a trash bag. Do you understand?" she asked.

I asked if she had a rake since that would be easier, but she said there was no rake.

"Go ahead and get started. I will be standing here while you work."

I started picking up pinecones because I didn't want to get in any more trouble. As time went by and I started getting tired, I looked back at her.

"LOOK DOWN! Don't look me in the eye, you have to focus. Don't let me see you looking up again or I will extend your time."

I didn't look up at her again. While I was working, she started talking to me and told me this would help me in the future and prepare me for the rest of my life.

"This will build you up," she told me, "so if you have to do this sometime in the future, it won't be new to you. You're going to be out here for the next three weeks, so you should get used to it."

Once recess was over, I dumped the trash bags in the dumpster and went back to class. I walked into class late and sweaty. The teacher had already started teaching, and no one asked where I had been. They only wanted to know why I was sweating so hard.

After a few days of this, my friends wanted to know what I was up to. When I told them I was picking up trash in the ditch in front of the school, I started getting picked on by everyone.

After a few weeks of work, the labor became more intense. I started shoveling dirt in wheelbarrows and carrying it around the school to fill in different potholes. Ms. Madison walked up to me one day while I was shoveling dirt.

"Are you enjoying this?"

I didn't say anything. I kept my head down and listened to her as I continued to work.

"I need you to understand," Ms. Madison continued, "that you're going to be doing this type of manual labor for the rest of your life. Next time, the punishment will be even worse when you're older. You'll also have other black young men doing it with you."

I kept looking down, working, and pushing my wheelbarrow full of dirt. Apparently, Ms. Madison did not have a problem reminding me of what she saw for my future and what she thought of me.

There was nothing I could do in this situation, and I was not in a mental space to fight back—or even determine if I deserved this type of punishment. I kept pushing dirt, shoveling, and making sure there was not a single pinecone or speck of debris on the ground.

My three weeks of community service were over and I finally could go back to recess and start playing again. That next Monday's recess I went back to play and just as I was about to swing. Ms. Madison came and tried to get me back out there to do more community service. I told her I was done—my three weeks were over and she said, "Oh wow, I didn't realize the time went by so quick."

CHAPTER 3
WALKING THE PAST

After school on Friday was my favorite part of the week. I liked it for the same reason everyone else did—no school for the next two days. I found an escape in my imagination and really threw myself into the world I created in my head. I was really good at drawing, so I would conjure worlds of robots, ninjas, and anything I could imagine. When I drew and imagined things I could dwell there for hours on end. Growing up you could walk into my room and see that every space on the wall was covered with drawings and graffiti of fictional imagery.

Late one afternoon I was in my room playing and my daddy came and told me I needed to cut the grass in the morning. I didn't know how I was going to cut the grass since the lawn mower was broken, but I was not going to remind him of that.

When I woke up the next morning, it was not because of the alarm or my daddy telling me to get up. No, I was awakened by the lawn mower I had thought was broken. I laid back down thinking that my daddy wasn't going to come in and get me. I thought that he was going to cut the grass himself. A few minutes passed by and my daddy came into my room and told me it was time to get up and work.

After I cut the grass, it was midday and my daddy told me to come with him for a ride. I was not nervous like I usually was because I was not in trouble at school and had been doing well. w

We got in the truck and started driving towards the direction of my school. I didn't know why we were going out there. As we drove, my daddy started talking to me and telling me about life and his upbringing. He started to tell me about his mother and father.

"Son, what do you want to do with your life?" he asked me.

"I don't know, Daddy. I haven't thought about it before."

"Well son, when are you going to start thinking about it? You don't have a lot of time, you're going to get older and before you know it, it's going to be time to live your own life."

He continued,

"Growing up in this town, I didn't have a lot of options for what I could do. Eating and picking cotton were the only things that mattered. My family picked cotton to pay rent in order to have a place to sleep. We were sharecroppers and that's what we did growing up, at least until high school."

I didn't understand what a sharecropper was, so I kept my mouth closed and just listened. When there was a silent moment, I asked my daddy how often he had to pick the cotton.

"We didn't just pick cotton, son, we picked anything that needed to be harvested for that time of the season. We picked cotton, corn, tobacco, soybeans, and potatoes. That is what we did all year long," he said.

After I got out of school, I had to do homework and then go outside and pick cotton. I couldn't take all day to do my homework either, I had to go outside and work. There was no fun time or leisure activity."

As we approached my school, we suddenly started slowing down. Then, we pulled onto the side of the road by the school and my daddy pointed to the cotton fields surrounding my school.

"This is where I used to harvest and where I used to pick cotton," he said.

I looked around

"Son, your grandpa was very aggravated and to me he always seemed to be mad and upset. He just wanted what was best for his family. The man was illiterate and didn't receive a lot of opportunities because of his education. He grew up during a very racist time; all he had ever done was work in the field and harvest crops. He also had drinking problems because of his troubles."

We got out of the car and walked across the street into the cotton fields. I will never forget the feeling when I first stepped into the fields of cotton that my father used to pick. I felt an emotional presence of sadness and aggravation. It was an unexpected burden that suddenly came over me. I didn't know what to do with it and it stayed there and it never went it away.

We started walking through the fields of cotton. Every time we stepped and kicked our feet forward to avoid from falling, dust and dirt would become unsettled and start moving. After a few steps, my pants were covered with dust and dirt. I walked a little further and I felt the dirt in my shoes. The ground was soft and as I kept walking, the back of my heels started hurting from lack of support in the ground.

I could hardly believe I was walking through the cotton fields with my daddy, watching and listening to him revisit the past that held him down. Watching and listening to him in the very environment that caused him subconsciously to always walk with his head down and never look into a man's eyes with confidence for a small portion of his life. While we walked, my daddy spoke to me about death and the idea that he was going to die one day, and that I was going to have to be prepared to live in a world that was not designed for me to succeed. He told me I needed to start walking confidently with my head held high.

My daddy started telling me how when he was a boy, the only thing he could do was do what he was told in order to eat and feed the family. One day while he was with his family picking cotton, he looked around and realized he was tired. Everyone was sweaty, aggravated, and tired. He stopped picking cotton and slammed his bag down on the ground. He looked at his daddy and said he didn't want to pick cotton anymore. My grandpa told him to keep working, but my daddy refused. Grandpa got up, grabbed him, and started beating him out of frustration.

"How can you run your mouth and say you are not going to do something when everyone is relying on each other to eat? The thought or idea that you even had an option was crazy. Talking back to your parents instead of doing what they say will not be tolerated."

The only reason my daddy did that is because he knew that there was a better way and he was speaking out of frustration and anger. No one had the answers or the way out of the situation. My daddy knew that no other kids his age were harvesting crops in order to have a place to sleep and eat at night. It was only his family that he knew of, so the frustration and anger came from wanting something more without having the means or ability to see how to obtain it. All he had was his family working in cotton fields with him.

We started walking back to the truck and decided to go get some food. It was hot that day and we needed a mental break from the emotional conversation. We decided to go get some hotdogs from Hardees; it was one of our favorite places to eat and it gave me a good opportunity to ask more questions and learn more about my family's history.

CHAPTER 4
USE YOUR HANDS

Food-there is nothing better than the idea of being able to eat. One of the worst types of pain is a hunger pain.

There were a lot of hungry moments growing up. What is more important than figuring out what to eat? It is figuring out how to eat. Understanding where the food is coming from is just as important as eating itself.

Getting off the school bus was always a pleasure because I knew that there was a Capri Sun waiting inside for me to slurp up. They were so good, and just like potato chips, you couldn't have just one.

After I had my snack, I had to go outside and work since I didn't have homework after school. I didn't get the opportunity to take a nap—that was considered blasphemous growing up.

Whenever I worked outside, it was always working on car motors or something else that involved grease, or cutting grass, or chopping down trees; the outside duties were my responsibility. At the time, I didn't understand why I needed to be out there, especially when I could be inside watching TV. The best shows came on in the afternoon, too. There were so many choices, such as *Hey Arnold*, *Cat-Dog*, *Recess*, *Rocko's Modern Life*, *Rugrats*, *Dexter's Laboratory*, and a few others. I wanted to be inside drinking more Capri Suns, eating snacks, and waiting on my momma to come home and give me a hug.

I was able to watch a portion of *Doug* on the TV. Fifteen to thirty minutes went by and when the show went off, I heard someone pulling up in the driveway. I heard the car turn off and the door close. The walls were very thin; you could even hear the door lock and unlock in the mornings. I didn't have to see who it was because normally my daddy just came in the house and would leave everything in the car. My momma always did the complete opposite—normally she took her time because she had to get all her things out the car like her Bible and things she needed to do at home.

I thought this time it was my momma getting her things since I didn't hear the door immediately close. I decided to wait and keep watching TV. Then I heard someone coming up the back steps that had a heavier step than my momma's. When the door opened, I looked back and saw my daddy.

Now, this isn't necessarily a bad thing. I was doing what I was supposed to be doing, and normally he would tell me to do some chores or something that I didn't really mind. I'd just take the trash out and put it on the back of the truck.

This time he walked into the house and didn't tell me to take the trash out, but instead told me to come outside with him. I didn't have a problem with that since I enjoyed being outside for the most part regardless of the weather.

However, today was not the day I would enjoy my usual outdoor activities. My daddy had the garage door open with his 1966 Plymouth Barracuda inside. The engine was running and it was idling in place with the hood up. I knew something was going on.

He told me to come into the garage and hand him a Phillips screwdriver because we needed to adjust the carburetors on the motor so it could run better. I didn't know what a carburetor was, and I didn't know how to adjust carburetors. I asked where the screwdriver was and he pointed that it was on the other side of the car. I reached over and handed him the screwdriver and then watched him adjust carburetors for the first time. I remember listening to the motor and hearing it idle up and down. The sound of the engine changed as he twisted one small screw. The sound of the engine seemed like it was running out of gas. When he turned it the opposite direction it was getting too much gas. One direction made it get louder, the other direction softened the noise. I couldn't figure out why it was doing that. I didn't even understand why we were trying to fix a motor that was already on and running perfectly fine.

Despite my confusion, I stayed in the garage with my daddy. A few minutes went by, then half an hour, and before I knew it hours had gone by and we were still doing the same thing. Finally, my daddy said we could call it a day. He walked in the house and didn't look back. I was tired and wanted to eat and give my mom a hug. After I finished eating, I went to bed and crashed.

The next afternoon the same thing happened. We went outside again and worked on the same thing. I was in the environment of mechanics and didn't know why I couldn't be inside watching cartoons.

We turned the engine off, crawled under the car, and started changing oil. It turned out crawling across the ground was one thing I could get excited about. Now that I was getting dirty, I felt like I was having an adventure. It was so cool to be able to see underneath the car instead of the interior of the car. On top of that, changing the oil was very easy. I just had to loosen one screw and all this black stuff would come running out. It was dark and very thick. I didn't know what the black stuff did to the motor or why so much of it was coming out. I just knew my daddy called it oil and needed to take it out. Once it had all run out, we had to crawl back under the car and put the screw back in. Then, we had to put some other fluid into the vehicle that had a light brown tint. He told me that it was oil. I looked at him and asked. "We just took oil out why do we have to put it back in."

"Well this is what helps the motor run smoothly so it won't lock up and break."

My daddy looked at me and asked,

"Do you like to eat?"

I thought that was a rather random and interesting question to ask because everyone needs and likes to eat.

I responded and said that I liked snacks.

"What about food like dinner and the food that your momma cooks every night?"

"Well, yeah that's good too, but snacks are great."

"Son, if you don't learn what I am showing you right now, you won't get dinner or any more snacks. If you learn how to work on a car, you will never go hungry. At some point, Jerome, you are going to have a family and they are going to want to eat too. Learning to work on cars is one skill that will never go away. Someone could walk up to you right now and cut your legs off and you would never be able to walk again. But if you learn and understand how to use your hands and fix things, you will always be able to provide for your family and yourself."

We needed to crawl back under the car that afternoon to adjust a few more things under the motor. I needed to hold up a few parts of the motor so they could get screwed in. It was hot under the car and I was very sweaty. There were clouds of gnats everywhere that wouldn't leave me alone. My daddy needed to screw in the part I was holding up, but I kept moving because the gnats were in my face. He said "Stay still son. Bite and eat them if you have to." I thought *well that isn't a bad idea—if I can't move my hands, I can move my head.* My daddy caught me trying to eat them and he sent me in the house and called my crazy. After I was in there a few minutes, he came back in and got me and said to come on back outside. I knew that he couldn't give up on me or what he was trying to teach me that easily.

We ended up staying outside that night until 11:00 p.m. before we finally went inside. I was too tired to do anything else except go to sleep and think about the fact that I didn't like working on cars and staying outside all night to do work. And I still didn't understand what it was all for.

I didn't know at the time that I was learning how to use my hands to create the things I wanted for myself. I was developing a way to think analytically and was work through things and building a process around them. I was still walking through the unknown simply doing what my parent's told me to do.

CHAPTER 5
THOMAS EDISON

In middle school, I was introduced to the people and bullies I would learn to know and hate. I would meet people from different areas in town that I didn't grow up with on the same street. I also learned skills like computer literacy that would carry over to the next few years of my education. Then there was the Accelerated Reader (AR) program where I had to read enough to get fifteen points per week in order to stay out of detention.

Research was required for certain classes like science because we needed to support or get information for different things we learned in class. Unfortunately, I didn't like to read books at all. I often found myself in detention for not reading enough to earn the appropriate amount of AR points and not doing enough research for class.

The day began as an ordinary day. Science was always the first class and it was also my homeroom class. There were always interesting things I enjoyed in the science classroom, It was always fascinated with the world and outerspace. I enjoyed traveling virtually to different places and seeing different things like on the Magic School Bus. We always had reptiles in the room such as turtles, snakes, and lizards. We often got to feed the snake at the beginning of class and we loved to watch it swallow its food whole. Then it was time for math. On this particular day, the teacher had something else to talk to us about.

"It's time to talk about the science fair!" she exclaimed with a smile. After passing out the papers and explaining what the science fair was, she walked around the classroom and gave recommendations for what project we should do based on skill level and aptitude.

I was one of students that needed to do a volcano and get my parents approval to help me with it. Everyone had to think of a something to build but doing a volcano was a good science fair project. When I went home that day, I told my parents about the science fair and asked them about the volcano.

Surprisingly, my momma thought it was a great idea and my daddy agreed.

At that time, the school system was determining our strengths and talents based on our science fair projects. I concluded that were judging our parents to see what kind of support system each of us had based on the quality of the project. Everybody passed, but our futures were being decided.

After I came home and said I wanted to build a volcano, I started developing and preparing for the biggest explosion anybody had ever seen. Since the science fair was going to be in a library, in my mind I imagined a few bookcases catching on fire because of a mistake I made and people running around trying to escape.

My momma started helping me with the volcano during the afternoons, and it turned out the volcano was doing great. The clay was hardening and everything was working exactly the way I imagined it. After the volcano was done, we tested it—baking soda came out instead of fire. It was nothing like I imagined.

After my momma and I were almost done, my daddy came and talked to me about how everyone was going to be building a volcano.

"Now that the volcano is done," he said, "Let's start on something a little more challenging that no one else will have."

I didn't understand what he wanted to do. I liked the volcano and thought it was cool. Besides, we were almost finished.

We came to an agreement where we would start something else and if we didn't finish it before the fair, we would showcase the volcano instead. If we did finish, we would pick which project to take to the fair.

I agreed and the next day my daddy put a sheet of paper in front of me.

"We are going to make a light bulb turn on," he explained.

I stared at the paper in confusion, not understanding how we could make a light bulb turn on with a piece of paper. Then my daddy explained to me we had to design the project in order to build it, and that was what the paper was for.

While he was talking to me, it seemed like he was speaking Spanish, because I didn't understand a word of what he was talking about. Then my daddy told me to draw a light bulb on the paper. I followed his instructions and started drawing. Next, he told me we had to draw wires for the input and output of the light so the current could travel from one direction to the other.

I didn't really understand anything my daddy was saying, but I continued to draw as I added a rectangle connecting one side of the light bulb to the other.

"Now you have connected the light bulb. What is going to power it? The light bulb has to have power in order to turn on," Daddy explained. I still didn't understand how I was going to make a light bulb turn on simply from the drawing since I didn't have a physical light bulb with me.

Daddy continued to explain that we needed to connect a power source in the diagram, so we needed to draw a battery and connect it into the wiring in the picture. After adding the battery, I thought I was finally finished. I was excited and ready to go play a videogame and do something I understood. But we were not finished yet.

"How are you going to control the light, son? Does the light in your room stay on, or can you turn it on and off? You need to place a switch in the circuit somehow in order to make it turn on and off."

Finally, after explaining to me how to place the switch inside of the circuit, it was time to call it a night.

The next night was interesting because we needed to design a box to hold all of the circuits, batteries, and light bulb. This task wasn't as hard. I was pretty good at drawing and drawing a box was really easy. It was a little more difficult to build the box since I'd never had to build a box with a sliding door before. After I glued all of the sides together, we needed to drill a few holes to place a switch on the side of the box.

Afterwards came the most difficult part—wiring. The picture I had drawn did not match what I was physically trying to do. My daddy just handed me a pair of wire trimmers and told me to wire it exactly like the picture. I sat there for hours trying to figure out how to do it, but could not make it work. I fell asleep on the floor while trying to get it done.

The next day I sat there again trying to figure out how to wire it. Daddy came and laid beside me and helped me figure it out. I was sitting there for a while and after he finally explained it to me a little bit more, I understood how to do it. All the nights laying on the ground doing mechanical work started to pay off. I could put a few things together with my hands. I was even able to process things better. Now I started to push the switch on and off and the light bulb worked like the one in the house. I thought it was one of the most amazing things I had ever done. I spent the next few days preparing my poster that would explain how we built the project and how it worked at the fair.

During the science fair, the judges walked around and asked us about our projects. They also gave advice about what we might be good at doing in the future.

When the judges got to me, they asked me what I had made and who had helped me with it. I smiled and answered their questions. I explained how we had built the volcano first and then decided to change and build the light bulb project instead.

At the end of the science fair, I received first place. This was one of the first times I actually won something or received first place. They said I would become an engineer in the future. I didn't know what an engineer was at the time, but it sounded good so I smiled, went home, and celebrated with my momma and daddy.

Figuring out how to make a light bulb turn on was pretty difficult. It required me to think things through and map out a plan. That was the only way I was going to get it done.

PART TWO

CHAPTER 6
I AM DYING

Everybody had his or her niche and that quirk that made him or her special. Everyone was under the same umbrella. We are talking about an education system where 79% of the students were going to get a high school diploma or GED and 15% were going to get a bachelor's degree or better. Where education is not a priority, but making sure kids were passed along to keep numbers high and at the standard was way more important than making sure they were equipped with the essential skills to succeed.

You could be the cool kid who everybody wants to hang around. Or the geek who withdraws to his own world. You could even be the brain who everyone thought was very smart; the star athlete who everybody else aspired to play like. The list goes on and the dynamics constantly change when you're in high school.

Then you had me—the guy who went through all of those things, but never really excelled in any of them. I was tall, skinny, and goofy and just didn't know what was really going on most of the time. I played football at the time and the team was having a winning season. It was like having VIP exclusive access to all the major parties, and the effort that was required to get good grades was very minor. You didn't really have to turn in any homework or even pay attention in class—all because you were an athlete.

In ninth grade, I decided to stop playing my favorite instrument, the trombone, in order to focus on football. I could not be in the band and be on the football field at the same time during the same season. I also wanted to start playing basketball, but my parents said that I could only play one sport because I had to work on motorcycles and cars during the off-season.

So-some days after school I would get off of the bus and walked two miles to work on motorcycles and anything else that needed to be fixed at the shop. Every day there was something different going on. I was often tired from football practice and heat exhaustion, so I would go use the bathroom and lock the door and lay down on the bathroom floor. After I rested my eyes a little bit, I would flush the toilet as if my stomach was hurting and go back to work like everything was normal.

This time of the year I was playing football and every day Coach Barnes would scream across the football field, "Do what you got to do, so you can do what you want to do. If you boys would just do what I say to do and do it correctly, we wouldn't be out here for so many hours. I want to go home too."

So, from the summer until the end of December we would have to listen to him say that to us, and nobody understood what he was talking about. And after practice I would go work on motorcycles, cars, and dirt bikes, you name it, I worked on it. If it had a motor I could fix it. Other days I had to cut grass at home or the shop.

This year was a special year because the football team had a winning season. This year our roster was full of Division I and Division II college prospects and everyone's goal was to go play college football.

All of our skilled players ran our 40-yard dashes in four and a half seconds or less. Everyone was squatting 375 pounds or more, and every skilled player was bench-pressing 250 pounds or more. When it came to potential and stats we were among the best in our division. Our record at the time was 8-0, we were undefeated. At every practice we did well, and with every game we won the goal of getting the championship ring got closer and closer.

We needed to play our rival school, Richmond Raiders out of Rockingham, NC, at some point and we were more excited about this game than any other. We needed to stay hungry to win this game but humble as well because we had other games before our rivalry. One practice at a time, one day at a time and one game at a time, that was the philosophy that was instilled in us that year, and it worked. So, after winning eight games in a row, the one that truly mattered was approaching.

Finally, the ninth week was here. Like us, our rivals were undefeated. After losing to them several years in a row, it was well known that this rivalry was the biggest one in the state. College recruiters were going to be there and if you played in this game you were definitely going to be observed for potential to play on the collegiate level.

October 28, 2008 was gameday, the entire school was excited. Everyone dressed in their school colors and represented school pride. We even had a pep rally that day. There was nothing that could bring us down—this was the year we were finally going to win.

All of the football athletes had half of a day of classes and the remainder of the day was spent in the fieldhouse going over plays and getting our minds together for the Friday night lights. The time went by very quickly. Everyone was listening to one of two things in their headphones, Young Jeezy, *The Recession* or Lil Wayne's *Da Drought 3*. They were the only two mix tapes relevant to us at the time. If you were not listening to one of those mixtapes, you were not considered to be serious about what this night was going to bring.

The sun finally went down and those lights turned on as the show officially started. The locker room was tense; no one was talking and everyone was putting on their equipment. We were excited, and it felt like we were really going to war to fight for our lives and what we truly stood for. This was the year we were going to do the unthinkable. Every year we would lose to Richmond—this was the year we were going to beat them. This was the year everyone was going to remember Scotland County's football season.

Nothing else in the world mattered now. Everything was on us; we carried the dreams of our families, our school, and our county on our backs. Time stopped in that moment when everyone was finally dressed, sitting in their locker waiting. All we heard was the crowd outside, and then our captain saying, "This is it men, stay focused. Concentrate on what is ahead of you, for there is only winning and losing."

Coach Barnes walked into the locker room and looked around. Everyone looked up and he said simply, "Let's go." Every one jumped up with a roar—you would have thought that it was a battle cry. Around us, the walls felt as though they were moving and time started speeding up. We stepped out of that locker room and everyone one was there, standing, waiting for the Fighting Scots to take the field for the most memorable moment of our lives. There was no sitting room left and the only standing room was in the parking lot. Seven thousand people that showed up in that stadium and everyone was anticipating a good game. The captain stopped us all and looked at us and said, "This is it, the moment we have all sweat, cried, and bled over. Now is the time to make an impact. We are the impact. We are the lions and this is our den. We eat or we starve, those are our options. Tonight, nothing can take us off this high. We are our worst enemy and tonight we play ourselves, repeat after me.

'When you feel that everything is perfect, and nothing can go wrong, fight harder.

When you feel that everything that can go wrong has gone wrong, never give up.

But oh lord, if I shall die.

Let me die as a true man.

But oh Lord, let me Never,

Ever, Give up.'

Scots on me Scots on Three,

ONE, TWO, THREE and SCOTS."

Everything made sense in that moment. We took the field and no one looked back because to look back meant failure. We returned the kick-off to the 40-yard line and the very next play we scored a touchdown. On the opening drive things were looking good for us Fighting Scots.

We went back and forth until we finally went into the fourth quarter with seconds left and we went for the touchdown and Richmond intercepted the ball and ran it back.

We went into double overtime and at the end of the game, Richmond beat us by one touchdown and we had lost one of the most important games of the season. After the game, everyone started crying and hanging their heads low. Coach screamed out in front of everyone.

"You bastards lift your heads up. Tonight is my fault, you have no reason to hang your head—you men played extraordinary. The man who hangs his head is the man who is ashamed, and you have nothing to be ashamed of tonight. I saw champions take the field. You have definitely proven your worth and value on this field tonight."

We all walked into the locker room sad and emotional, everything we had ever known to be true to us we threw on the table and bet it all. Everyone started throwing their helmets and shoulder pads around the locker room from aggravation and anger, thinking back trying to figure how or where we went wrong.

Everyone sat around exhausted and started getting their things together to go home for the night and relax for the weekend. My momma called me and asked where I wanted to meet her to pick me up from the football game and I told her across the street from the school. There were so many people out that we were never going to be able to get in and out quick enough, and being stuck in traffic was never fun in such a small area. I was trying to make sure that my momma would stay safe because there were so many people, which made the possibility of something bad happening that night higher than usual. I was walking through the school trying to get to the other side, closer to the front of the school where I told my momma to meet me. She was waiting for me in the neighborhood across the street. There were so many cars that traffic was backed up all the way to the stadium and it seemed like it was not moving at all.

I was finally approaching the main road where I would cross the street into the neighborhood where my momma was waiting on me. So instead of crossing the street at the cross walk, I decided to walk a little farther on the side of the street I was currently on. I figured I would cross the street when I was closer, or better yet, when I had her in sight. The traffic was still at a standstill in the ongoing lane, but there was not much of any traffic at all in the oncoming lane. So, I looked to my left—there were a few cars coming—I looked to the right to make sure traffic was still backed up and not moving.

I started crossing the street and as soon as I reached the middle of the road I heard a horn. I looked up and there was a car approaching me very quickly. I took one step and I realized my body would not move and I didn't know what to do or how to react. I tried to move back to the safe side of the street where I came from, but I couldn't move fast enough. The car was directly in front of me now and I was in the middle of it, staring it in the face as if I was a deer in headlights.

I heard the brakes squeal. Then I closed my eyes. BOOM. The car lifted me off of the ground and I was in mid-air, floating for what felt like a few minutes— it seemed like things were going in slow motion. My eyes were closed and when I opened them, I was looking in the sky and all I could see were light reflections showing in the night sky. I knew the car had just hit me and I was not dreaming. BAMMMMM! I immediately closed my eyes again and came falling down. BAMMMMM! I hit the hood of the car. My hands reached up as I covered my face. There was this loud shattering noise. I felt glass breaking on my body. I felt as though I was being stabbed in my forehead and back. The car finally stopped moving and I rolled off the side of the hood and hit the ground and just laid there. Noises that I heard very clearly were not loud anymore; all the screams and shouting started to sound like whispers. I started tasting crunchy grains of sand in my mouth. My vision was getting dimmer, things that were once colorful were a shade of red and the lights that were once bright turned into circles of bokeh. Lying there on the ground I saw blood in my hand and I was dying.

CHAPTER 7
WALK WITH A LIMP

I am dying, I am dying. My eyes were shut and I couldn't hear anything at all. Then I started hearing a voice in my head that said, *"Get up, get up, get up! If you stay here you will die, now GET UP."* That is all I remember hearing in my head while lying on the ground. My eyes opened, my adrenaline rushing, I didn't feel any pain. I reached for the car that was parked beside me and lifted myself off of the ground, but then I fell. I didn't have any balance. I started to lift myself off of the ground bracing myself one foot at a time. I was finally standing on both of my feet looking around. I was confused and everything was blurry.

I looked at the car, the hood was bent. The entire windshield was cracked I looked down and my XXXL t-shirt was no longer white—it was red. I could not see out of one eye. I was dizzy, but I was standing. I could not figure out why my shirt was red though. I saw the ambulance in the distance towards the school and I said, "If I stay here I am going to die. I have to keep moving, I can't stop. I have to make it over there to the ambulance and get help."

So, I started walking. I just kept walking and didn't stop. I heard people asking me, "Are you alright?" I responded, "I am fine." I heard people rolling down the window yelling, "Why is his shirt so red?" I just kept walking until I got to the place where I saw the ambulance, but then I looked up and realized there was no one there. I saw the lights from all the cars. I looked down again and my shirt was still red and it was wet. I rubbed my head. I could not figure out what was going on, this was one of my favorite white shirts and it turned red. I brought my hand down and my hand was wet and red I knew my head was bleeding and blood was gushing out the side and running down my face and neck to my shirt. I placed my hand back on my head to stop the bleeding.

I just kept walking. I saw another ambulance farther in towards the school where traffic was backed up even further. I needed to walk in order to live, that was the only thing going through my head.

I heard someone say, "Jerome, Jerome are you okay it is your cousin, are you okay? Do you need help?" I looked and did not recognize the face so I yelled back, "I am going to the ambulance, I can't stop!" I started moving faster and faster. I hear a voice.

"Jerome come back."

I never stopped moving. I finally reached a man by the ambulance and said, "Hey, can you help me?"

He said "WOAH, what is wrong?"

"My white shirt turned red and I think I am bleeding."

"Sir where are your shoes? Why are you barefooted walking around?"

I turned around and pointed in the opposite direction, I did not know I wasn't wearing shoes and I did not know what happened to them.

He said, "Just sit down right here on the ground."

He went over to the ambulance, then came back and asked me about my parents and I pointed to the opposite direction. After a few minutes of sitting on the ground this man came over and said "Lay down flat on the ground for me; we are about to take you to the hospital. "How many fingers do I have up?"

I said, "You have up two fingers."

"How many do I have up now?" he said

"You have up five fingers."

He said, "Let's get him inside and ready to go, on the count of three we lift. One, Two, Three, LIFT!"

Once they lifted me up and placed me in the ambulance, they asked me for my momma's number and I gave it to them, managing to type it into someone's cellphone. The next thing I knew, we were driving and I heard the sirens from the ambulance. I started going to sleep. I was so tired and the gentleman said, "You have to stay up for me, you can't go to sleep, do you think you can do that?"

"Yeah." I replied.

I started dozing off again so he said, "You have to stay up, how about you talk to me, tell me about yourself." So, I started talking, not knowing what I was saying, I was just following instructions.

We arrived at the hospital and they put me in an emergency room and I just laid there. Then a nurse came in and cleaned me up from all the blood and changed my clothes. She placed me back into bed and I just laid there and fell asleep. When I awoke, hours later, I saw my momma and daddy sitting in my room waiting on me to wake up. They came over, gave me a hug, and asked if I was okay and I looked at them and said I was. I was not okay, I was scared and I started crying. I started apologizing to my momma and daddy. They said "It's okay. What are you apologizing for?"

"I know that our family is struggling and the ambulance is going to be expensive. I have to sit in the hospital and get treatment. We cannot afford any of this stuff. And it is all my fault."

My momma replied and said, "Baby it is not your fault, don't worry about this, we will be okay. In life things happen. You stay focused on getting better and as a family we will get through this. You understand me? We will be okay. Come on, close your eyes and let's pray."

'Dear heavenly father we come to you in a time of need asking for strength to endure. We ask that you heal Jerome from all the pain and suffering. Heal his mind and body. Send your angels from your kingdom to come down and stand by his bedside and watch over him. Keep him safe, I pray that our family supports, guides, and reinforces our tolerance so that it will endure this storm and the ones to come. In the name of Jesus, we pray, amen.' Now son don't you worry about nothing else okay? Get you some rest."

I felt a soothing, rush of calmness come over my body. I didn't worry anymore, my head stopped hurting and then I feel asleep. I did not know how powerful prayer was until that moment. There was an immediate release of pressure and tension that I had and I felt better. Later on that night, they put staples in my head and bandaged me up and wrapped my head to keep it from bleeding. The next few hours I sat in the emergency room sleeping, and I remained there resting and eating the ice cream until the next day. That morning the hospital released me to go home. The nurse assisted me in a wheel chair that morning and said she wouldn't be able to finish the football season in tiptop condition. I sat at home the next three days loathing not being able to play football and changing bandages on my head. I had staples stuck in my head and they had to stay there for the next two months.

One day, I went to check the mail box and I found a ticket in the mail for jaywalking. My momma came home and I told her about the ticket. She said we would take care of it. Then said, "Jerome you have to go to school tomorrow. I know you don't want people to see your head bandaged up, and yes, they are going to pick on you, but you will be okay. And sometimes in life we have to keep moving forward even when we don't want to. You remember when you would get sick in school and I would tell you that you would still have to go? Well this is the same thing, you still have to go, but this time you have to face the music of your situation and I can't come get you out of school either."

I was very depressed and I didn't want to go to school. I knew I was going to get picked on and looked at no matter the location I went to. That Sunday, my aunt Wanda came and got me and said, "I heard you lost your shoes."

I said, "Yeah, those were the only shoes I was getting for the rest of this year, so yeah I lost them, I only have one to be honest, not sure where the other one is."

"Well lift your head up, it's over now and everything is going to be all right. This is what I want you to do, go around the corner and pick you out some shoes from my neighbor house. She sells sneakers and you can pick you out some so you will have some new shoes to wear for school."

I walked down there and got myself some air force ones, the low-top kind, all white. That did something to me on the inside; it felt good to know that I had someone who supported me outside of my momma, daddy, and sister.

I dreaded the next day. My momma woke me up and took me to school like normal. We drove up to the school and she said, "Have a good day." And I got out of the car. I started walking inside and everything felt okay, I didn't feel like there were any eyes on me until I walked through the door and all my friends asked me if I was okay and what had happened. I had to explain the story all over again.

The bell started to ring and it was breakfast time and everyone was getting off of the buses to go get their chocolate milk and super donuts—super donuts were a quintessential morning delicacy. The donuts could fill the cafeteria up with a smell that inspired you to have a great morning. When you walked into the cafeteria, it felt as though everything started to align because of the welcoming sensation you received from having an amazing breakfast. This morning, however, was the complete opposite. I felt all of these eyes looking at me; I felt my body twisting from being nervous and uncomfortable. I decided to get in line as quickly as possible and get my super donut so I could leave and go to my classroom. As I stood in line, someone walked up to me and asked what was wrong with my head. All I could say was a car hit me and she started laughing and walked away. I started getting sad on the inside. When I walked out of line towards the door and as I walked past all of the tables I heard everyone asking what was wrong. They were laughing at me, pointing fingers, making jokes, and using my condition as an outlet of entertainment.

This continued for the entire time I had that bandage on my forehead. I tried to go to practice and be in the atmosphere I loved so much, but my coach told me to go home because I wasn't of any use to him standing around. It was very difficult to hear that. It was hard to understand how I could be of no use to something that I loved and enjoyed to do. The sport that I had always loved and wanted to play, I could not play anymore. This was a hard pill to swallow. I didn't get to finish that football season because of my head injury. I would have random headaches and pains. As time went on it became evident to me that I kept getting picked on and looked at with smirks and slanted eyes while walking around school. When I rode the bus in the afternoon I would normally sit in the back, but now I stayed near the front for protection. If someone started picking on me the bus driver would hear them and she could stop them or they would be disciplined.

Going to school every day was a hassle and a headache. It was something that I dreaded doing and did not enjoy. If I could have stayed home until I recovered, I would have. Lunchtime was the worst. I started sitting by myself. I didn't talk and no one would invite me to sit with them. I isolated myself and stayed secluded. There were a lot of things that were going through my mind. I decided to sit by myself in isolation because of the way people were treating me. I helped everyone place me on an island. I allowed my condition to determine my position and attitude, not realizing or understanding at the time that everyone has his or her unique problems— we all walk with a limp.

CHAPTER 8
DAMMIT I FELL

Three months after being hit by the car, I was still healing and just started hanging around my friends again. I did not have to wear that bandage across my head anymore, and that was a good thing to start feeling normal again. I was able to live without having someone look at me strangely and laugh all the time. I had just finished taking and passing my driver's test a few weeks before, so there were limits to what I could do with my driving. I could only drive from five in the morning to nine o'clock at night, this was normal for someone who just received his or her license. It was a normal Saturday and I had been working at the motorcycle shop all day and finished up late in the afternoon. I went home, took a shower to get ready for the night, and normally my friends and I would go sit in Burger King and play spades all night until it was time to go home. Tonight, was one of those nights.

There was nothing special about this night. It was 8:30p.m. when everyone started leaving, so there was plenty of time for me to get safely home. I lived about fifteen minutes from the Burger King in town so driving back home was not a problem. Driving home listening to music, I was a little nervous because it was already 8:45p.m. and I was trying to follow the rules and get home before 9:00p.m. I was driving on a two-lane road, cars coming towards me as I'm passing them. I was looking out in front of me and I noticed a car was passing another car far in the distance. This was normal on 401 South, it has always had pretty moderate traffic. When I looked back up I saw there were a lot of lights, but these lights where coming towards me instead of driving beside me. In an instant I knew that there was a car driving in my lane and I had to avoid a head on collision. Everything started moving very fast as if someone pressed the fast forward button on a remote.

I grabbed my steering wheel with both hands and turned to the right to drive off the road. I was driving in the dirt and I needed to get back on the road; all I could hear were rocks hitting the underbody of my car. I turned my steering wheel to the left and I felt my car twist in the back and start drifting a little bit, so I pulled the opposite direction to try and get the car under control. The back of the car started to fish-tail and I was turning the steering wheel the opposite direction of the way my car was fish-tailing. For a second I got control over the car, but my steering wheel was still turned to the left, so I drove through traffic into the next lane. I felt my car turn, but it started to turn too much and I felt my car lift off of the ground and into the air. I held onto the steering wheel—I knew I didn't have any control and it felt like I was being lifted in the air by a crane. I knew I was in mid-air when I opened my eyes and I was upside down in the car. The front of my car smacked the ground and I instantly closed my eyes. I let the steering wheel go and immediately I started hearing the car smash, glass was breaking. I covered my face with my left hand and grabbed the seat belt and pulled it tighter with my right. I felt my knee get stuck under the steering wheel. I was going in circles I knew this was it and I said, "GOD help me."

The car stopped tumbling. I had my eyes closed still. I started dropping as if I was falling backwards and I didn't know where my support was coming from and I felt the back of the car hit the ground one more time. Once I opened my eyes, I was upside down and there was dust and dirt everywhere. The top of the car was smashed in and was only a few inches away from my head. The airbag never deployed. I was stuck in my seat belt, but I knew that I could not stay in the car, I had to get out. I didn't know if the car was on fire and leaking gas and if it was going to explode or not. I started thinking *what do I do? What do I do?* I tried to bite my seat belt, thinking that maybe I could chew threw it, but that didn't work. I started trying to rip it and pull it apart with my hands like paper, I was strong enough right? *Dammit.* That didn't work either. Blood started rushing to my head, I stopped and started looking around, analyzing the situation. I was upside down in a flipped car. If I placed my hand on the roof of the car and press the seat belt button I could slide out and down the seat using the back support and not hit my head and fall unconscious. I did just that and it worked; I dropped down from my seat that I was tangled in all while upside down now I had to find a way out of the car. The front was smashed in, so I couldn't have gone through any of the front windows. Everything was crushed, however, the back was still intact. I crawled through the small inlet between the seats. I tried to open the door, but couldn't do it. I covered my face and started kicking the window and the glass busted; once I turned my body around I crawled out of the car.

I started walking towards the side of the road and sat down and just looked at the car. I didn't have my phone or any way to contact someone for help. Then, this minivan pulled up; I couldn't tell what it was exactly, but it had emergency lights on it. This older gentleman got out the vehicle, he had blond hair and was wearing shorts and a short sleeve polo nautical shirt. He was a volunteer patrol officer. He asked me who was driving the car and I said I was.

"How did you get out?"

"I crawled out."

He said, "Okay just stay right here."

Suddenly, you would have thought the whole police department, emergency rescue, and all the fire trucks that Laurinburg, NC had to offer showed up. My momma then showed up and said, "Thank GOD you okay." My aunt Wanda showed up next. A police officer walked over to me and started questioning me about what had happened, when I told him he said, "Okay." and that he would be right back.

He came back a few minutes later and said, "Sir we are going to have to test you for alcohol usage, could you please walk on this yellow line? Could you please blow into this tube? Could you please follow my flashlight?" The test just went on and on. I passed them all. He later asked, "Are you sure that is what happened?"

"Yes, I am."

Now I was upset because no one believed me. You don't leave Burger King and say, "I'm going to flip a car tonight." The gentleman who drove the minivan said that he hadn't seen any cars coming towards me in my lane, explaining that he was a just few cars behind me. I looked at this man and started walking towards him. My momma grabbed me by my left hand and pulled me back and I said, "You also were not in my car, so you really don't know what was in my lane do you?"

"Young man, I didn't see any cars, that's all I'm saying."

I started walking towards him again and lifted my right hand at him, but my momma grabbed me and wrapped her arms around me. The police officer walked away and he returned with a reckless driving ticket. I put my head down and lifted it back up and asked him why he was giving it to me and I told him I didn't deserve this. My momma grabbed me and said, "Come on, it's okay, everything will be okay son, let's go home." I grabbed my face and started crying; I could not figure out why everything was happening so fast. I didn't get why I was just hit by a car 3 months ago and now I flipped the car that my parents had just finished paying for after seven years. I just started feeling normal in school again now that I had my head wraps off, and now this happened.

Why didn't anyone believe me? Why was I made out to be a liar? What was wrong with me and why couldn't I do anything right? I fell asleep when I got home and my momma woke me up the next afternoon. She said, "Wake up son, it's twelve o'clock." I got up and went to go sit on the couch and watch cartoons. Momma walked in the living room where I was sitting and said, "Come here. I need you to drive to the grocery store and buy some bread."

I looked on the counter and there was a fresh pack of bread already on the counter top.

I said, "Momma there's some bread right there."

"Jerome, I need some more bread, do what I said."

"I can't drive though momma."

"You will be alright son. Here is the money for the bread. Go to the Wal-Mart and get it."

Wal-Mart was a lot farther than the gas station. I saw my momma looking at me through the kitchen window. I was so scared I started crying in the car, but I could not go back in the house without the bread. My sister did that once and it didn't turn out well. So, I had to leave and I went on my way. I made it back home after a little while. Next day, my daddy told me to drive thirty minutes away to get some parts for a motorcycle. I was still shaken when I got behind a steering wheel. I believe that month was the most errand running and driving I've ever done. After about a month, I was comfortable behind a wheel again and I was not scared anymore. I was still a little nervous, but not scared enough to cry at the sight of a steering wheel.

CHAPTER 9
MEND WHAT IS BROKEN

Dammit this is crazy; how did I get into this again? I just sat there looking straight ahead. I put my head down and then I inhaled and exhaled. There were no tears coming from my eyes. It was only anger because here I was in another familiar situation. Three months after the second incident I ran into the back of a red Nissan truck. I sat in the car in awe trying to figure out how to get out of this situation. While waiting on the police to come, I thought about the idea of driving off. That would only make the situation worse than it was, so instead I just sat there. Finally, an older woman got out of the truck and walked over to my car and asked if I was okay. I told her I was.

Well, it turns out after we looked at her car in comparison to my car, I definitely ran into the back of the truck. There was definitely damage done and the truck's tailgate was bent in pretty bad as well as the bumper. My bumper and hood were bent in and my radiator, now smoking, was broken as well. The police arrived and gave me yet another ticket for reckless driving.

This was all the easy part—I think I had been mentally prepared and I had seen and spoken to enough police officers at this point that it had become really easy to deal with them and seeing blue lights in my rearview mirror. It has become less difficult to have people drive by looking and staring at you while you're in the middle of a bad situation. The hard part, on the other hand, is calling my daddy and telling him I got into another car accident and ran into the back of someone. However, at this point I had to and I had nothing to lose. I couldn't go home with the car like this. So, I made the phone call. My daddy answered and he asked me what was going on.

I said, "Daddy I got into another car accident and I ran into the back of someone."

He hung up the phone.

Then after a few minutes he called me back and asked, "Where are you?"

"I am downtown Laurinburg, across from the unemployment office."

"I will be there in five minutes." He said. Then hung up.

After about ten minutes, he showed up, looked at the car and said, "Dammit son how did you do this?"

To be honest, I didn't really know how I ran into the back of that car, so I said what made sense and told him.

"Daddy, I had mashed the breaks to slow down, but my foot slipped off of the pedal and before I knew it I couldn't bring my foot from underneath it and I ran into the back of the car."

Well he looked at me and said, "Well dammit son you had to be going about thirty-five to forty miles per hour to do this. How fast were you going?"

"I don't know."

"You don't know?"

My daddy looked at the police officer and said "Police officer sir, Police officer. How fast do you think you would have to be going to cause this type of damage?"

The police officer responded "At least thirty-five to forty-five miles per hour."

My daddy looked at me and said, "Thank you sir."

He shook the police officer's hand and said, "Let's go son, get in the car and follow me."

The car was overheating because of the broken radiator and I needed to drive it back to the house.

So, we started driving and I followed my daddy on all of the back roads, through places that I'd never seen or been. My car was smoking and it was as though I was driving around with a fire under my hood. It felt like the car could blow up and stop at any time. If I stopped I knew that I would be stuck on the side of the road but there was nothing we could do. I knew that we couldn't afford to get the car towed by anyone; we needed to keep driving and make it work.

We finally made it back to the house and my daddy just looked at the car. After a long conversation, he looked at me and said, "You're going to fix my car and everything else that you break, mend what's broken. You're the mechanic, fix what you break and keep fixing the things you break. You may even have to fix something someone else breaks."

The following week my daddy purchased a new radiator for the car and brought it to me and said "You gon' stop breaking my shit, take this and go use what you know to fix it. Whatever personal problems you are going through, figure it out while you're fixing my car." That morning my momma woke me up and said, "Time to get to work. You need to go take care of that car and get it running again." Everyone agreed and I had to use everything I learned so far to figure out how to handle this situation without guidance or instructions.

I started working on the car and after a few days of working, I fixed it and I got it back operating and running correctly. There is this old proverb that says if something happens once, it will never happen again. If it happens twice, it will surely happen a third time. When you're leaving a problem, another is followed right behind it. Even when you are going through a lot of things in your life it is important that you fix your problems, that is what the mechanic does. That's what physicians, doctors, and therapists do too. They are constantly chasing after the solution to solve the true meaning of problems that are in front of them so they can mend what is broken. Fault and responsibility do not go together. It is not my momma and daddy's fault that I got into so many car accidents, but it is my responsibility to fix my problems and handle the emotions that come with them as well.

CHAPTER 10
FROM SCRATCH

It was my senior year in high school and as a senior you needed to provide a senior project that everyone could judge, view, and look at. For some reason our senior projects needed to be done and finished in my English class. It turned out that whatever class your homeroom was in, that was where you had to build, develop, and create whatever it was you were going to present at the end of the year. These senior projects determined if you were going to graduate or not. There were no group projects—we all had to work as individuals. Everyone spent their time during this period talking and trying to figure out what they were going to do for their projects; however, the other portion of the time was spent goofing around and laughing.

We had the most amazing teacher. He simply said, "Do something you enjoy and something you don't mind standing in front of others and talking about. If you can do this doing the project will be easy and you won't be stressed out by it. The project will seem like a breeze and if you run into a problem it will be fun to solve." So naturally, that concept went completely over our heads. As a class we had no idea what we were going to do. During the class, the teacher decided to take us to the library twice a week or so to do the research because he knew that we were not going to do any research on our own time.

Research was required for certain classes like science because we needed to support or get information for what we were going to talk about. It turned out this was no different. We discovered that after asking enough questions the project required us to write a five to ten-page essay with supporting information. So we needed to come up with a topic and have it submitted to him in two weeks, and it was the only thing we could think about.

Two weeks passed and I decided to do a project on the samurai, the Japanese warrior. My teacher asked me why, and I told him I always had a fascination with Japanese culture and that I collected katanas as a hobby and all of my favorite shows had something to do with swords and karate. He looked at me and saw the passion glaze over my eyes and just looked at my smile and smiled back and said, "Go for it."

After everyone in class received approval to proceed with our projects, we goofed around for most of the time in class—talking and playing around for the next month. Then, one day the teacher walked into class and told us there was a deadline to have a certain part of the project done and it was next week; we needed to have a rough draft of the paper done and finished for his approval.

I started doing research immediately. I learned so much in a short time. There was so much to read about Japanese culture; the dedication it took to make one katana. The discipline that was required and craftsmanship took years to accomplish and learn. The most intense portion was heating the steel and folding the steel to create something that would not break—there are ten thousand layers of folded steel in one blade. It takes days to create one katana. This was so fascinating to me. The level of devotion it takes in order to accomplish one goal. I always knew that Japan was the one place I wanted to go. I didn't know how I was going to get there. I didn't even know when I was going. I just knew I had to go and live among the people, thrive and see the level of devotion that the craftsman was applying to his work of art - his masterpiece.

Soon the last few weeks and final decisions on our projects needed to be made. We only had a month left and we needed to be finished with everything and be ready to present. Judges would decide how well we did and whether we were going to graduate or not. We were all sitting in the library and everyone was silent trying to use printers and add the final touches on their projects. I printed out my paper and it met all the criteria. I was finished. I walked over to my table and looked at it and the poster I had done. I felt a feeling of relief that I was finally finished with something that took me weeks to accomplish, but I was not happy. I was not satisfied with this; I wanted to change my entire project. I wanted to do something different that made me happy. I wanted to feel astonished and amazed and I wanted everyone to be in awe. I wanted everyone to look at my project and never forget what I had done. I wanted my project to be talked about for some years to come and I wanted it to be undeniable that mine was the best project out of everyone in the class of 2009.

I came to my teacher after doing all of the research and learning so much about the place that I dreamed about more than any other place. And I told him I didn't want to do it anymore.

He looked at me and said "Jerome it's Monday, you have two weeks, you can't change now. Why are you going to change? You have a finished product."

"Well, I am not satisfied with it and I don't want to do it anymore."

"Well what are you going to do?"

"Well I am going to build a motorcycle from scratch."

He looked at me and raised one eyebrow with a look like *what the hell is this kid talking about.*

"Wait, so how are you going to do this? You're going to build a motorcycle, like one that you ride with a motor and everything?"

I said, "Yes, I can do it I just need a little time and I will show you."

He said, "How about this. You go ahead and try and if you don't succeed, keep what you have so you have something you could fall back on."

I walked away with a smile on my face and excited because I knew I was about to blow his mind and everyone else's.

I went home that afternoon and told my momma and daddy what I was going to do and they both smiled and said, "We have the tools to do it and there is your motorcycle frame to get you started." And momma gave me a hug and said, "You do what makes you happy and do whatever it takes until you're satisfied."

The next day after school I started working on my project. I saw the motor that I needed but it was all in pieces and I asked my daddy to help me. He said, "Well, get started and I will be over here working if you need me, but this is your project. Get started, that is the only way you're going to get finished."

So, I started and in about two days I had a completed motor sitting on a workbench ready to be placed on the frame of the motor. This was crazy because I had always worked on pieces of the motor, but never the whole thing. I went home to tell my momma what I did. I ran into the house excited and screaming.

"Momma, Momma."

She said, "What boy?"

After I told her what I had done, she said, "It is only showing you that sometimes you need to understand the pieces of the puzzle in order to really put them together to make the whole piece."

I smiled at her and nodded my head to agree and said, "uh huh." I kept moving, smiling, and running around the house—what she said completely went over my head.

The next day it was time to place the motor on the frame to get it started so it would crank up and run properly. That's when I needed my daddy's help, I could not lift the four-hundred-pound motor by myself. After I asked, he came over and helped me bolt it into place and then he walked away again. We had a customer show up, but I had to wire it up and make sure that all the wires were connected together so it would communicate appropriately to the different mechanical parts.

I was working non-stop it seemed. To get this done I had to put all of my effort into it and I had to grit my teeth and wipe the sweat off of my face and replace it with the oil on my hands. I was looking at a finished product and I finished days before the deadline.

I was done typing my paper as well and my momma had to edit it for me. After I finished the paper and the motorcycle, I had to go to school the next day and ask my teacher if I could bring my motorcycle to school and he said he wasn't sure and that I had to go ask the principal. I walked to the principal's office and he was not there. I walked around the school looking for him—I didn't come this far to get denied at the very end. Once I found him I explained the situation to him. He agreed to let me bring my motorcycle to school. The following week my daddy and I drove it up to school in the trailer and unloaded it.

I got security to open the back door for us so I could push it into the classroom. Once there, it sat in the corner all day, and everyone you could think of walked by the classroom to see the motorcycle. It was a phenomenon because no one had ever done it before.

There were so many questions like how, why, who did this? Towards the end of the day it was time for my presentation; by that time majority of my classmates had already presented. I tried my best to go last because I was afraid to talk in front of crowds. I was so nervous drops of sweat began to pop up on my forehead.

I walked up slowly to the front of the classroom, unsure of myself but I made it and started talking about how I built my motorcycle Overall the presentation needed to last for five to ten minutes and that unnerved me.

At the end of the presentation everyone clapped for me and I rushed back to my seat. It was so funny because I started out doing something completely different just to start all the way over to use one of my strengths that I already had. Sometimes you need to start over, it gives you the opportunity to reevaluate and adjust. I wanted to do something that

I was interested in. What you want to do does not always best represent the things that you need to do. Even when what you want and what you need are both positive, they are not equally beneficial. Starting over helped with that, it gave me a new approach and exposed a new option for me. A few days later I received my score and they gave me a 99. *I looked at my score and said where is my one point? Now what could have possibly cost me one point? I guess nothing is perfect and there is always room to get better.*

PART THREE

CHAPTER 11
SMILE, SCHOLASTIC SCHOLAR

I finally made it to College. I was enrolled into Richmond Community College. I was older and wanted to explore a little more, but I was scared to death of change. Leaving high school on a good note was nice, but I didn't have the highest grade point average to get me into any of the other schools that my friends were going to. My closest friends were very smart; they were attending Howard University, North Carolina State University, or some other, but I was going to a community college. It discouraged me to see all my closest friends go off to school—I felt stuck and left behind. They never made me feel inferior, but inadequacy was a constant lingering feeling. I had high SAT scores, but I didn't apply myself, and my grade point average was low—I didn't think I was smart enough. I decided to trust and listen to my parents when they said it would benefit me to get an associate's degree before entering the workforce. It would prepare me better, considering I didn't do too well in high school. High school didn't prepare me to go to college either, so this would be a good step regardless of what I thought. I figured that any step I could take was better than none at all.

College was great. Everything was going well—I managed to enroll in as a mechanical engineering major, and it was only going to take me two years to finish it and graduate. Richmond Community College was a great school; the environment was bright and engaging and there were modern brick architecture buildings on every part of campus. The grass was green at every stretch of landscape. There was an overwhelming openness that you felt when you drove up to the campus; It felt welcoming rather than intimidating. It seemed like the campus could go on and on with the small number of buildings and open fields of green grass everywhere.

My first few days of school were great. I was meeting new people, and I didn't see anyone I knew in high school. I had to make friends with the people I met in class. I was a little scared though—I didn't know what they would think of me, and I didn't want to be awkward—so naturally, I sat by myself, speaking when spoken to. Often, I would sit around and wait for someone to talk to me.

I was able to go to class, meet the teachers, and see who I was going to be learning from for the rest of the semester and I had a few good classes for my first time being in college—they seemed very easy and that turned out to be the case.

One day we were encouraged to participate in different extra-curricular activities because it would help us with our growth. Maybe I walked in with my expectations too high, but none of the clubs stuck out to me. I remember people talking about clubs like archery, fencing, bowling, and things that were exciting. There wasn't any of that at Richmond Community College. It was all boring until I saw a group of black men standing in suits who seemed very intimidating, smart, and articulate. They had a presence about them that I hadn't yet seen on campus—they caught my attention. I walked past, glancing, trying to see what it was all about while trying to appear uninterested. I couldn't make out much of the sign, but it said, 'something male.' So I walked to the end of the hallway and acted like I saw something more interesting. Then I turned around and walked past the table again.

A gentleman at the table, an unatractive young man, looked at me. His beard had dandruff in it, and you could tell he didn't wash his face too often and—to top it all off—his breath didn't smell nice either.

He had on a suit though, and when he spoke to the other men, they listened. The presence that he carried was very genuine and true in nature. When he spoke to you there was not any reservation in his voice, and you heard reassurance. "Excuse me my name is Marcus I saw you walk past the table the first time and look." I replied, "Nah bruh, you didn't. I was trying to find the business club." I knew that there wasn't a business club—at least I hadn't heard of one. So he said, "Well I thought you might be interested in what we do as an organization."

I walked over.

He said, "I am the president of the Minority Male Mentoring Program. We are the only student organization that focuses on the enhancement and growth of men that look like you. If you were to join this organization you would be surrounded by men like yourself that have already gone through the classes you're in. They will be able to help you develop and become a better student and man. Does this sound like something you're interested in?"

I wasn't ready for the question, so naturally, I said yes. "So, what is your name?" "Jerome John." "Okay Jerome, we have our meetings every Monday and Wednesday at 4:30pm in this room right behind us. I will see you there, okay? And, it's business professional the first meeting." "Okay," I said, walking off with a handful of papers. The next week came and it was time for the meeting. I walked in and there were about twenty young black men there that came to join the organization. The room was quiet. I knew everyone was nervous to be there; it was unlike anything I had seen before. The only places I was used to seeing black men in suits were school, church, and funerals. Then the program started right as I sat down. We began with ice breakers. We introduced ourselves I felt myself sweating because I was laughing and enjoying myself. There was a lot of good energy that day and it stayed that way. I enjoyed myself in there and before we left the president, Marcus, challenged us to start wearing a tie and slacks every day to school to separate ourselves from everybody else. That way, when people looked at us it was easy to recognize us as part of the Minority Male Mentoring Program. This was going to make other young men want to be a part of something that was bigger than themselves. The goal was to encourage the young men who were not in that room. We wanted to invite them in and help them become better as well.

From there on out, I decided I would dedicate myself to this and I would wear a suit, or a tie with a button-down shirt and slacks, every day. I invested my time into making sure that I looked nice. Once I began doing this, others started noticing me and taking me more seriously. I was going to classes and there were moments when I was called out among other students because of how I presented myself. That following week there was a presentation in class. The professor was an older gentleman in his eighties. He called everyone out and asked them to stand up and introduce themselves. He slowly made his way down the roster, looking up and down, connecting each name with a face. When he finally got to my name I didn't hear it at first because I was obviously, thinking about something else entirely. He called my whole name out, "Jerome Lee John."

He looked around the room—I raised my hand and just smiled at him. He looked down at the paper, looked back at me, looked down at the paper, and then looked back at me. He said, "Jerome, I'm not trying to be funny or anything. I'm not trying to come on to you, but you have an amazing smile. When you smile it's pleasant, and there's a feeling of pressure being lifted off when I look at you."

At that moment I just kept smiling—I was embarrassed really, and didn't know what to do or say other than thank you. Then he kept talking about it and he said, "Class, look at that smile—isn't it amazing? My smile has never been that great and I've lived a full life. Let me tell you something, Jerome. Your smile is going to take you places your credentials won't allow you to be. Now that I have gotten that off my chest, stand up and say a little about yourself."

The next class period he called my name and looked at me and I was smiling, and he smiled back and said, "Man, that is just great." It wasn't until later that I realized there is a perception that you give other people based on how you carry yourself. Presenting yourself well will take you a long way.

Three years had gone by. I was in two-year program, but because of the way classes were offered, it took an extra year. I found myself participating in the Minority Male Mentoring Program full time. I was not on the Executive Board, we all called it "E-Board" for short, but I did stay a constant and active member who had a lot to offer, and was willing to go above and beyond to build the people around me.

I managed to grow and develop through this community college, but now I was at the stage where my time was ending, and it was time I started looking towards the future.

My counselor, Daphne Stancil, was one of the most amazing spirits I had the opportunity of meeting while in school. I would walk into her office every day, unannounced, to see what she was doing and to talk with her. There were pictures everywhere that cultivated creativity and growth. She had many degrees on the wall, and in front of those degrees you would see her standing there with open arms and a welcoming smile on her face that spoke to anyone that entered. There was always an abundance of love in her office, so much that you noticed the difference once you crossed the threshold.

She spoke to me quite often about going to continue my education at another institution. I was always listening, but there was always that feeling of ineptitude. I didn't know what I would do or how I would get there. I had always wanted to go to a university even back in high school, and I knew that if I had a little bit of help, I could make it happen. I told Ms. Stancil this and she said, "Well don't worry. I will help you and walk you through step by step."

She handed me a piece of paper with a website that would link me to a scholarship application. I was hesitant at first because I had never filled out a scholarship application before. Getting exposure is important when you are trying to do things you have never done before. With this application I had the potential to be awarded $750 to help pay for school for a semester. It was not a lot of money, but I was grateful.

A few months later, I received an email stating I was being awarded the money and I didn't know how to feel. I had been turned down so many times—getting that one yes meant everything to me. I couldn't sit still. I kept thinking about going home to tell my momma and daddy.

After I finished reading the email, I packed my things up and walked into Ms. Stancil's office and told her. She smiled and said, "Okay, next we need to work on what university you are applying to." I already knew the answer that—North Carolina Agricultural & Technical State University. I was bouncing around with joy and happiness. I walked quickly to my car and went home for the rest of the day. With bigger things to think about, I skipped my classes that day.

The following week I walked into Ms. Stancil's office and she said, "We need to get you to Agriculture & Technical State University. I have a college buddy that works there—I'll call him right now to see if we can set up a tour and get you admitted." She started typing on her computer really fast, looking for his phone number on the school's website, and finally found it after about five minutes. She picked up the phone and made a phone call to her friend who turned out to be an admissions counselor. She spoke with him and he offered me a private tour of the school right then and there. All I needed to do was drive up there.

I went home and told my momma about the good news. She said she would take the day off so she could go with me. A few days went by and the excitement was still there, but I didn't know how to tell my momma that I didn't want her to go. It wasn't that I didn't want her there, but I felt like I needed to do this on my own. I needed to leave Laurinburg for the first time without help—to travel the world and see for myself what it had to offer. I was nervous, but I needed to do it for me.

The next day I went to my momma and asked her if it would be ok if I went on my own.

She said, "Why, are you okay?"

"Yeah, I'm fine. I just need to do this on my own. I appreciate you wanting to be there, but I have to do this by myself. I have to grow up and step out there on my own at some point."

After a few minutes of talking she said, "Well, you can go up there, but not in your car—you need to drive safe. So, you take my car, and I will take your daddy's car."

Wednesday came and I drove to A&T State University. I drove two hours North on highway 220. I looked into the distance—I was stunned and paralyzed. It was my first time seeing skyscrapers. The traffic was heavy. I was driving so slowly that there were people blowing their horns at me and speeding around my car. I drove into downtown in six-lane traffic trying to figure out where I was headed. I finally saw my turn on East Market Street. I took the right and drove through the center of downtown. I couldn't see the tops of the buildings; people were walking though construction not adhering to the signs. It was bizarre and mind blowing.

I drove up and started seeing signs for North Carolina A&T. I pulled into the school, and all I saw were brick buildings and stretches of inviting green grass as far the eyes could see. It felt as if it was a bigger experience than my current school, but I felt like I was home again. Something inside was telling me that this was it. I drove into Webb Hall's parking lot and that's where it all started for me. The Admissions Office was on the basement floor of the animal and science building. I walked through the hallways, finally found the reception desk, and asked for Mr. Cromartie. After waiting for five minutes, he came walking extremely fast around the corner to greet me. He was a dark-skinned man whose height stretched to six feet, five inches, who, from the moment I met him, talked excitedly about A&T.

He said, "Look Jerome, I didn't graduate from A&T, but I can tell you about this school better than my alma mater. This is an amazing school. Quite honestly, it is the greatest, historically black college and university in the world." He looked at me and smiled.

"Let's go, I hate it in here. We're going walking around campus."

And so we did. I saw the Aggie Stadium, its accents of blue and gold. I saw the student union that had been there since the 1960's. I was introduced to the reflection pool—a pool where aggies go to reflect on the hard and difficult times, to see where they come from, and to get an understanding for where we are. There was a memorial at the reflection pool that showed bullet holes from when the army came on campus in the 1960s and started shooting. He showed me the Greek plots on campus. There was so much to see and absorb. I literally could not take it all in. After the tour he looked at me and asked, "Now Jerome, can I expect your application to be coming to me?"

I succinctly responded, "Yes."

After a few weeks, there was an award ceremony where they passed out the plaques for the scholarships, and students were given the opportunity to shake the hands of the people that donated the money. After leaving the ceremony, I drove back home and walked across the street to the mail box, finding a letter with my name on it. I didnt normally get mail, so to get some was a shock. When I realized it was from the admissions office, I froze a little bit. I knew that this was the letter that was going to tell me if I got accepted or not.

I received a phone call from a reporter who worked for the Laurinburg Exchange newspaper—they wanted to feature me on the front page of the newspaper as a successful student. I don't think my smile could have gotten any bigger. Constantly losing and feeling like it was never going to stop. I was finally winning and it was back to back. The reporter and I scheduled a time to meet and discuss my education and my plans for the future.

"What are you studying?" The reporter asked me.

"Mechanical engineering with a concentration in mechanical drafting."

He was quiet for a moment.

"What do you want to do with that?"

"Well I potentially want to get a good job working for a good company."

He said, "Okay, is that what you want to do after graduating from Richmond, or do you have other plans in mind?"

I responded, "Well, I actually plan on going to North Carolina Agricultural and Technical State University to study Information Technology."

After he asked me a few more questions, he asked if we could take a photo. We set up a few of my books that I used during my studies and after positioning them correctly we took the photo. A few days later there was a story that came out in the Laurinburg Exchange news paper and I was being featured on the front-page. It read, "Scholastic Scholar," along with a blown up picture of me and my books.

After a few months of working and going to school it was finally time to graduate—everybody was anxious and excited to be graduating from college. There were some who had been there longer than they may have wanted to, but they were finally accomplishing their goals. I learned that it doesn't matter when you reach your goals because there is no time stamp when it comes to being successful.

With the rush to purchase the expensive cap and gown and making sure last minute grades were turned in, the last few weeks before graduation had been stressful.

Graduation was Saturday at 9:00 am. Everyone was excited and ready to move on to the next phase of their life. Everyone had to line up in order based on last name and wait at the door. The doors finally opened for the graduates to walk, and I felt this rush of silence that started from the front of the line and flooded all the way to the back. Then the master of ceremonies said, "Spring 2012 graduates please stand." Music played as we walked in. I followed in line accordingly and found my seat. All the graduates took a seat, and the ceremony finally began. Once the master of ceremonies began the introductions I felt my eyes get very heavy—I became too comfortable and relaxed in my chair. I closed my eyes expecting to just rest them for a few - moments just to get some energy so I could enjoy the ceremony.

"Rise class of 2012 you are now Graduates of Richmond Community College." My eyes opened, confused, trying to figure out why everyone was shouting. Everyone was standing up and smiling. I heard people screaming and whistling. "Please, class of 2012 turn your tassels. You are now alumnae of Richmond Community College." I realized at that moment that the graduation was over and I slept through the entire thing. *Okay*, I thought, *now I just need to find my parents and take pictures, then we can go home.*

That afternoon, I went home and fell to my knees and prayed, meditated, and cried. I made it and there was nothing anybody could do to stop me. I graduated from college. I felt a sensation and spark of energy that came over my mind and body. It seemed to say, *get up you still have so much farther to go and still so much to accomplish.*

CHAPTER 12
FIND YOUR VOICE

My palms were sweating. I couldn't quite squeeze the podium like I wanted to—the sweat just kept making my hands lose grip. I was standi6ng there and my breath was heavier than normal. Squeezing the podium was the one natural thing that felt normal. I started to lift my head up to keep from looking down. It was really hot all of a sudden. *Dammit I knew I should not have come up here.* That was a few months after I had finally gotten comfortable being at A&T.

It was a good thing to have a roommate that was from my area. He was easy to talk to and get along with. We lived in one of the dorms suites F - one of the nicer buildings on campus. There was a dorm right across named suites E. At first, I didn't know how the suites got their names, but from a sky view you could see they were built in the shapes of "E" and "F". Classes were not that bad. I transferred in from another institution so I came in with a few credits. I was basically starting from the beginning because I was a mechanical engineer, and when I got to North Carolina A&T I changed my major to Electronic Technology, which later changed to Information Technology. I had to fulfill the major classes and the math and science requirements. My first classes that semester were Micro Computer Applications, Quantitative Fundamentals, Unix/Linux, and Calculus. They were all fairly and introductory classes. How was I going to navigate this campus and excel in them more than just grade-wise? First, I had to figure out what clubs I could join, so I went looking around trying to find those clubs that were fascinating like archery or the athletic clubs. After walking around looking, I couldn't find anything. After being in school a semester, I realized that I missed the organizational fair at Richmond Community where they would showcase all the organizations and clubs. I wanted to get out there and do something. I wanted to do more than just go to class and go back to my dorm. I'm from a small town without a lot to do, but I knew I had to do something different. I was walking through campus and I saw a flyer that said NAACP talent show. I saw a date and it said auditions were coming up that same week. I told myself I was going to be there.

The day came when it was time for the audition and I was nervous. My feet were going numb, but I left my building to walk into Pride Hall for an audition. Once I walked in, I only saw a few people. There were two girls name Nkenge and Brittney. Nkenge was short with hair that went to her shoulders—she was very nice—maybe too nice. Brittney was also very short, but she was more laid back and relaxed. There was this Indian guy sitting in the room across from them who wore a khaki suit that was way too tight. He looked a little uncomfortable. The pants were hugging his knee cap and I could see his thigh breathing. He introduced himself and said, "Hey man, my name is Ike." Then Nkenge wasn't so nice anymore. She screamed across the room, "No your name is Isaiah Maggett." Then she looked and started smiling again, and I just looked and thought, *yeah I knew she was a genuine person who was very honest.* Isaiah looked and said,

"Yeah man, you can call me Ike." After all the introductions Ike asked, "So who are you?" I introduced myself and told them were I was from. Brittney looked at me and said that sounds country. Where is that?"

"It's an hour south of Fayetteville."

"Oh, okay, cool."

I knew she didn't know where that was either, so I left the conversation alone. After sitting there for a while, they asked why I was there and I told them I was there to audition for the talent show. They were all in awe because they said the flyer didn't get approved for promotion so it wasn't supposed to be posted—they were going to have to reschedule it. The auditions never happened and they were never rescheduled.

I exchanged numbers with Ike, though. I had a good feeling about him. He gave me such positive energy, but it seemed like a calm energy as well. He said he was going to reach out to me about a few programs they were going to have in the future. It felt good to go to an audition to meet new people even though I didn't audition. At least there was something that came out of it. I started to engage with my peers who already engaged in the same things that I wanted to do. Later on that month there was an audition for the gospel choir for a pantomime opportunity. I could sing, but I was more passionate about pantomiming. I needed to bring two songs and needed to dance to both. I was going to blow them out the water. I was best at this. During the audition I gave the host my CD, waited to get called up, smiled, and gave it my all. Everyone clapped and they seemed to have enjoyed it. Now I just needed to wait a few weeks for them to decide. I was confident they were going to pick me. During the audition everyone was excited to know who I was and they were telling me how well I did. I didn't mind dancing as long as I didn't have to start talking. I was not a big talker, and I didn't like speaking in front of people. After the audition I realized that this was only my first semester, and I was starting to meet a lot of people and step outside of my comfort zone a little bit.

The next day I was walking around campus and a lot of thoughts started entering my head. I realized what I was doing was great; I was placing myself in new arenas and new atmospheres, but I was still doing the things that I was comfortable with. If I would have auditioned for that talent show, I would have mimed. I needed to grow and expand into territory I had never been in before. What do I need to do? What can I do? Who do I need to speak to or go see? All of these were important questions that I did not have the answer to. I needed to understand and find out who I was and what I wanted to be. There was so much going on around me that it was beginning to get hard to navigate. I knew that with distractions and so many things coming from multiple directions - school, family, and social activities it would be hard to find the answers to those questions.

I was lost in thought for a few minutes as I was walking past the book store. As I did, I noticed this guy who stood about six foot eight inches or so. He was probably the tallest guy I had ever seen in person. He walked like Donkey Kong from the video games. He was, however, dressed in a very nice suit. He walked with a purpose and carried a messenger bag with him. When I saw him I wanted to speak, but I didn't. I figured I could just admire him from far away. Who knew that this guy would later become my best friend? As he walked by, I thought back to when I wore shirts and ties every single day. Maybe it was time to pick it back up again and start dressing professionally. I remember something my momma told me—that people will judge you within the first thirty seconds of looking at you. She always says, "You're on an interview at all times." That is what kept going through my head. That following week my momma sent me twenty dollars to buy food. I was straight you couldn't tell me anything. I was going to go to the mall and buy a shirt or two. Waiting at the bus stop I heard someone say something about a thrift store where you could buy clothes. I had never heard of a thrift store before. Did not know what it was, but I listened to her explain it so I got on my phone and looked one up. I saw one, "Value Village," right by the mall and that was where I was headed.

I finally made it to the thrift store and I could not believe the smell. It was almost as bad as walking into the fish market for the first time. I grabbed a random garment and the clothes smelled like this to. I walked around the store with my nose flared up. I did not understand why things smelled this bad. After being in there a few minutes I became used to it. I looked around the store for about a half hour or so, and I saw a nice grey blazer for two dollars. I tried it on, and to my surprise, it fit perfectly. I knew this would be a great start. I never washed that blazer. Dry cleaning would have eaten up my $20 that needed to last two weeks, so I just sprayed some Febreeze on it and called it good. A few days passed and I wore my blazer everyday and changed shirts and shoes. Every day I wore a new outfit with my grey blazer, and I started to get a few compliments. I even received a phone call from Ike who told me there were executive board positions for the NAACP. *Here we go again.* The last time I received an opportunity like this I shied away from it because I didn't see where I could add value. He was the current vice president at the time. I asked him what I had to do. He said I had to give a speech, and I immediately got quiet and my eyes were big. I didn't know what to do or say, so I just said, "Cool." And I didn't think about it anymore. I just asked for the date and time. Once off the phone I started thinking to myself.

How in the hell am I going to do this if I've never had to give a speech before? What am I going to talk about or say? I called him back a few hours later and asked what I had to talk about. I had been racking my brain for a few hours now, not knowing what to say or how to start, or what position I was going to run for. He simply said, "Run for Mr. NAACP of the organization. This person stands up and presents information for the organization and host events. You are the face of the organization. You also, more importantly, organize the community service projects and end events. You need to speak on what community service events you want to bring to the chapter." So, I said, "okay." He said to go to the library and start writing, and that he'd look it over for me if needed.

I went to the library a few days later after thinking about not doing it at all. I needed to be prepared just in case I did decide to build the courage to go speak in front of all of those people. As I sagged in the library writing my speech, I realized that I did have a lot to say, I just didn't want to say it. My speech covered about 75% of the paper. I called Ike again at 11:00 pm, and I told him I was done with my speech. He asked how I felt about it and if I needed him to look it over. He then said, "Speeches are tomorrow—are you ready?"

I simply said, "Yeah, I'm ready.

That was a lie.

I wanted to tell him I wasn't sure about my speech, and that I really had no idea what I was going to do up there. But, I had been raised understanding that "I don't know," was never the correct answer. Despite my response, however, I think Ike could sense my uncertainty.

He said, "Yeah, it's okay. The most important thing is to go up there and be yourself. I can tell you pretty much what everyone is going to do."

My ears perked up.

"They are going to go up there and stand behind the podium and pull a sheet of paper out of their pocket and begin to read off of the paper. When you go up there, don't read off of the paper. You should engage the audience because that is what people need. When you want to make an impact they need engagement. Speak with intention based on what you wrote down, or even better, what you can do. I listened, said okay and as I hung up the phone, thought, *He crazy and out of control I'm not doing that shit!*

The next day came quickly—before I knew it there were only a few hours before it was time for me to give my speech. I sprayed some extra Febreze on my suit I got at the thrift store. I walked up to the building confident and ready. When I walked in, there were a few people there just setting up the event. As the time got closer my arm pits started to sweat. My nervousness started getting worse—but it was too late now—quitting or turning back was never a trait I held. Ike walked up and reached his hand out to shake my sweaty one, smiled, and asked if I was ready.

I only knew Nkenge and Brittney at the time. I had one guy walk in that was my competition, his name was Kevin. He was very well-spoken and likeable, and if I was not mistaken, was on the previous executive board as well. Even though none of that mattered it did to me; it psyched me out a little bit. So, I decided to go to the bathroom and to wash my face and hands. As I was washing my face and hands I looked down and I noticed my hands were shaking and I squeezed them to try and get them to stop. They wouldn't. I looked up in the mirror and I was smiling.

Even though I was smiling I was truly living. *This is what it means to live in the moment,* I thought. *To be in a situation where something so simple is tearing you apart and making you afraid. I have to use my voice and make someone listen and hear me, understand what I am saying. I have to utilize something I have always thought was small and ineffective.*

I left the bathroom and went back into the auditorium. There were twice as many people as before. I sat back down, nervously waiting. The program finally started a few moments later. After the purpose of the meeting was stated, we started with the speeches. The speeches were given in a reverse hierarchical format—starting with the secretary and ending with the president. My speech came before the candidates for vice president and president. As I was sitting there I realized every candidate was doing exactly what Ike said they were going to do. They were reading off of the paper and never looking up, standing behind the podium the entire time. No one looked up to project their voice.

When it was time for the candidates for Mr. NAACP, I didn't want to go first— I needed more time to get myself together. Thankfully, Kevin opted to go first. He stood behind the podium like everyone else and pulled out at least 3 sheets of paper as he spoke for all of the five minutes that was given to him. After he was gone everyone gave him a loud clap, and it really seemed like he had it figured out. He was going to get the position.

It was finally my turn and it seemed like I was stuck to the seat. My feet were heavier than normal. It felt like each step was going to be the moment my heart was going to burst out of my chest. I walked up and stood behind the podium like everyone before me. It felt safe back there. Even being there trying to squeeze the podium, it seem liked if I could just squeeze it tighter it would make all the anxiety go away. I started to lift my head up to keep from looking at the crowd and looking down. I began to get really hot, and the sweat on my forehead started to bead up. I wanted to clear my throat, but couldn't. It would have been so awkward. What was I supposed to say after doing something like that, "excuse me?" It was only a few seconds that went by, but it seemed like hours. Then as I was taking my paper out, things seemed to slow down.

There was a moment of stillness and silence that arose inside of me. All of the noise inside of me was quiet. All doubt and underestimation was gone for a moment. *You cannot possibly know the path should take if all of the attention is focused on things that do not truly matter. You never know the possibilities ahead of you if you never look forward. Be yourself unapologetically.*

Those thoughts came and went. I looked out at the crowd of people, and I started speaking with my country accent and tried to give it to them as strong as I could get it. I didn't care if the articulation was good. I spoke and words came out.

I started folding my paper back up to put it back into my pocket.

"Hey how is everyone doing today? I had a speech prepared.

I am not going to talk about what I wrote down though. I was going to stand up here and tell you about all the different types of community service I could do. All the different ideas I had for programs. I am not going to talk about any of that. The truth is I have never done community service and I don't know the first thing about it."

I started to walk around the podium to get to the other side.

"I want to speak to you all about who I am and what I can do. Not what I want to do, but what I can do. Firstly, I'm from a small country town called Laurinburg, NC, and I'm a transfer student. There are a few reasons why running for this position is important to me. I need exposure and I feel like this opportunity can offer it to me. I want to be developed and why not be a part of an organization that prides itself on helping people. I learned by just being associated with a few people in the room that you don't always have to know what to do. As long as you're willing to ask for help, someone will help you. I am willing to do for other people what was done for me. I cannot promise you I am going to be the best Mr. NAACP, or that I am going to provide the most amazing opportunity. I can promise that I will assist and provide support with any goal that we as a group decide on. I am running for your 2012-2013 Mr. NAACP. Thank you. "

Everyone immediately started clapping and smiling at me. I scurried back to my chair. They asked us to leave so they could discuss and vote. Once I walked out, I realized that it's okay to be yourself. I needed to be the best and purest version of me I possibly could. People were going to have to accept me for who I was. I decided to live unapologetically. Ike came back outside to get us. We walked to the front of the room. I just looked around and the announcement was made, "The next Mr. NAACP is..."

CHAPTER 13
MENS ET MANUS

It was my junior year at North Carolinas A&T now, and I had a few classmates that worked on campus and did a work study in career services. This is the same department that hosted the career fair. They told me to apply for a position in the office to work with computers. They knew me pretty well, so I had word of mouth on my side. The hiring manager, Mrs. Basheer, called me in for an interview a few days later and before I knew it I was hired for the job. I was not only going to have the opportunity to work with the team that hosted the career fair, but I got first pick on which employees to speak with. I got to make an impression on the recruiters.

At this point I did not like school. It was difficult, long, and I realized that high school didn't prepare me for this at all. I realized I was not good at taking tests. I knew that I could do the work, but I had to prove it through the means of taking a test. Everyone was judged off of their test taking ability instead of being able to apply what you're being tested on. There's something about a test that just really throws me off. Then I started doing some research on why testing was important and what was the history behind it. I learned this when I was Mr. NAACP.

I found that testing was designed and used to access a student's level of achievement and success. I found out that one of the first literary tests, administered between the 1850s and 1960s, were administered to prospective voters to test their literacy in order to vote and was part of the voter registration process. These tests were all used to deny suffrage of African Americans. After learning that, I became a little more aware about the institution we call education. I felt the this system was not designed for my best interest. I considered dropping out and going back home, but I felt there was a reason for me to be here.

Jawari, the same goofy tall guy that I saw wearing suits and walking through campus in my first few months at A&T, had become my best friend. He didn't know at the time but he really inspired me to open up to people and become friendlier. I had thought that the only people that I could count on I had left back in my hometown. He showed me another side of relationships that I otherwise didn't know I could create. So, after living together for two years, we had become very close and confided in one another about everything. We did everything together from partying and drinking to opening up our apartment to anybody that needed a roof.

Jawari and I were thinking about how to become better at what we do in school. We were both struggling with our grade point average, which reflected in our ability to get internships. Jawari was in the kitchen eating as usual—he always ate when he was stressed out. While putting cheese on everything, knowing he was lactose intolerant, he said, "Jerome, the best part is you already have a degree and something to fall back on. You're good with your hands."

I already knew that, but I was not applying it. I needed to be reminded of it. Him saying that made me remember that I needed to use my hands to create whatever it was that I wanted.

I went back to the drawing board to figure out what I could do to make a difference. I knew that I needed to create something, I just didn't know what. I didn't have the grade point average, but I did have time. A career fair was coming up and I was determined to get better results than before. I didn't have any corporate experience, so I decided to have project-based experience. I decided I could do projects that would involve me building something, like a website or building a server you could access from anywhere. There were all types of things that I could do that truly matter in this degree. It made me remember something I learned reading about the history of this institution. Mens et manus is Latin for mind and hand. That is the statement this school was built off of. Using your mind and your hands to create something. I worked day and night to build websites from scratch and learn HTML. I stayed up to make sure I knew how to host a website on my own server.

I was also volunteering to do graduate research with graduate students. I did it for free, but I learned a lot and I gained experience. After months, I had three or more things added to my resume. I was also president of an organization. I helped establish another organization on campus, and I was one of the university photographers. I was everywhere and doing everything. I was ready, my GPA was not amazing, but I had everything else. I could communicate and market my strengths and truly control the conversation. I developed a little charisma. I was more confident than I had ever been before.

As I was walking up to the gymnasium where the career fair was held, I was not nervous; there wasn't anything that could stop me. I walked in, registered, and began talking to employers from John Deere, Cisco, Altria; every company you could name was there. I was prepared to walk up and speak to all of them. Every company representative said the same thing.

"Jerome your resume looks great. I love the kind of experience you have. I like that fact that you have a lot of leadership roles and by talking to you, I can tell that they really helped. The only thing is your GPA— it's not high enough."

I walked from table to table only to be told the exact same thing at each one. To me it was either yes or no. My question was simple, *are you going to give me this opportunity or not?* At this point in my collegiate career, I had been to all of the careers fairs and had been told no at every single one of them. At this point, I had become accustomed to getting told no. I learned that if they told me no, I hadn't lost anything at all, I was in the same place I was in before I asked. If they said yes, I gained everything.

I walked over to the last table that I planned on visiting that day. I told the representative there that I wanted a leadership or managerial role in the company. She looked at me and said I would never get that straight out of college or for a starting position. That I would have to work for at least three to five years before I could do it. I asked her if she was a manager and how long she had been working there. She told me three years.

I realized that she was not happy with where she was and might have been trying to push those feelings onto me. She might have even been trying to tell me what she thought of me and where she believed I might end up. I left the career fair again without any opportunities. A month later the Thurgood Marshall College fund was coming up, and I applied and was turned down for that as well. Even with me working at career services, I never received an opportunity—not once. It almost seemed as though nothing was working, even with me working for career services and surrounding my self with the right people and placing myself in the right circles.

Later on that semester, I received a phone call from my momma as I was walking to class. She told me the woman that helped raised me died—my grandma had passed away. I heard her say that and I was confused because I just saw my "grandma" and gave her a hug. "She passed away last night," she said. I felt like a piece of me was just taken away and it was not coming back. Aside from my mother, she was truly the only woman I really loved. The one that I talked to, making sure she could see me walk across the stage after I graduated. The woman that was supposed to meet my future girlfriend. She was gone. I told my momma okay and I fell silent. My best friend Jawari walked out of our apartment and we started walking to class. He was just talking and kept talking. I didn't hear a word he said. He looked over at me and said, "Jerome, you okay you look like you're sick."

I told him my grandma passed away and she was the one who helped raise me. He gave his condolences and I simply said, "It's okay man, that's life." It wasn't okay though, I suppressed all of my feelings and I never addressed them. I failed most of my tests that week. I got drunk a lot that week and a few weeks after trying to make the hole in my heart go away. It never did fill back up. I never spoke to anyone about it either. I suppressed and it kept it all to myself. I simply forgot about her death as if it never happened.

I changed my perspective and I refocused on something else that could work for me. I needed a change of plans and a new mission that could build and enhance me as a young man. My childhood dream started to erupt in me again and I imagined myself in Japan. We had a study abroad program, but I didn't have the money. I started looking up the cost and realized it was way too much money, but I couldn't let the cost deter me from at least starting. I didn't have the luxury of looking where I was and not looking any further. I had to let the denials and roadblocks roll off of me. I never gave myself the time to address my emotions, but I knew I couldn't stay. I needed to find something that could change my focus. So, I went to the Office of International Programs to see what I could do.

A few days later, I moved and I met with a study abroad office advisor, and we talked for an hour. She talked to me about how there was so much money out there for study abroad and that students often didn't take advantage of it. I told her I was wanting and ready to go to Japan. I've always wanted to go and experience the culture and see what it was like. We laughed, we joked, and had a good time. She told me that I could apply for a scholarship after I was approved and accepted into the program. So after a few weeks of applying and making sure my applications packets were together, I submitted it.

Waiting for my results was the worst. I was feeling some anxiety—it was hard looking for a program that I qualified for. After waiting two weeks, I received an email saying I had been accepted into the study abroad program. I was accepted into Ritsumeikan Asia Pacific University.

I was so excited to tell people I was accepted into my study abroad program. When people asked me what school, I said, "I don't know it starts with an 'R' though. It's in Japan." Everyone laughed. It was amazing to me how opportunities arrived in my life. To not fit the standard in the system I was expected to survive in, I constantly created opportunities for myself. I needed to adjust how I was looking at my situation to a panoramic view to see all around me to make better decisions. In order to see what was available at all times and continue to chip away and carve out the door that was designed for me. I had the tools—I just needed to use them. I knew that I was in a system that was not my best fit. I needed to learn it and figure out how to place myself inside of it so it can keep working. I learned to take the situation I was in and make it work for me.

CHAPTER 14
STRETCH YOUR WINGS

It was my last semester at North Carolina A&T and it was finally time for me to do the things that would preserve and maintain the future version of me without any distractions. I decided a long time ago that I would conquer this time in my life, exceeding all expectations for what someone had for me and what I had for myself.

It was spring semester and it was time for me to make game winning moves and decisions. I had a friend tell me once that in chess there are masters that can, in 1 or 2 moves, place you in checkmate and win the game. I needed to make a checkmate move. I had done everything there was to do on this beautiful campus of mine. I needed to do something I was afraid of, something that would shake me up and take me to a place to solidify me.

My birthday was coming up and normally I never did anything for my birthday. I never would for various reasons—no money or nothing on my mind that I wanted to do. Something came over me and I wanted to go skydiving. It hit me square in the face one day as I was sitting on the couch watching cartoons. I am not sure what called me or had risen up in me to chase this particular ambition, but it became important to me. I needed to act on it. If I didn't do what was important to me or follow such a strong feeling now, I felt I would never do it. I didn't know anyone that had gone skydiving. There was no one I could reference or call. I needed to live outside of my comfort zone in order to fly and soar farther than I imagined.

I decided I would persist—the only thing that can come out of doing something you have never done is a valuable lesson. I didn't know anything about skydiving, but I did know that military personnel do it and others do it for recreation. So, I used the money I was making at career services and paid for my reservation. I didn't really tell a lot of people; this needed to be something I did on my own. I knew I was going to get something out of this, something that I was going to be able to look back on and tell someone about. I was afraid and nervous, but having that feeling wasn't a good reason to avoid the task entirely.

It was February 27, 2016—it was my 25th birthday. I was excited and calm, trying to maintain the thought that I was about to go jump out of a plane. I walked outside with bag in hand and got on the road. I couldn't sleep the night before. I was very restless. I needed all my courage. I was afraid, but I acted anyway. The drive to Wake Forest, North Carolina was long, but worth it.

The drive up was long and I was driving through parts of North Carolina I had never been before. The GPS on my phone finally said I had arrived. I was in the middle of a field. I knew I was in the right place when I looked up and all I saw was a group parachutes floating down from an endless sky. I kept driving and I kept looking up while smiling from ear to ear, excited about what I saw and what I was feeling.

After I checked in, I waited about two hours for my opportunity to get suited and go through the five minutes of training about what to do and how to handle different situations in the air. I honestly didn't hear any of what he was telling me. I was too anxious and nervous; I was sweating down my armpits. My guide for this experience was smiling at me. I was expected to literally trust this man with my life. It was time to go up in the air, They asked me what I was doing there and why I was sky diving without friends. I simply told them that they were too scared, so they didn't come. That was not the truth. I just didn't want her in my business. I needed to do this for me. We walked up to a plane that was not very big and was pale white with blue stripes on the side. I was the first one to climb on, and they said I should go on first so I could be last to jump. I walked in the plane and there were just two wooden benches you needed to place in between your legs.

Once everyone was on the plane, we started to take off. Once the plane lifted it began to shake. It shook until it reached the correct altitude. Once we arrived at the correct altitude, I heard a loud door sliding and the sound of it being forced open. The wind hit and slapped me in the face. Then this stranger behind me asked me if I was ready. *Of course I'm not ready.*

"Slide forward," he said, "Let's go." It was strange having this stranger encouraging me and pushing me forward. Then we got on one knee at the edge of what feels like the end. I looked out and around—then looked down. I was afraid, I really didn't know what was going to happen. I was looking down at what seemed like an endless void 15,000 feet in the air and my first thought was, *how did I get here? What am I doing up this high?* Then he said in my ear, "We are going to go on three." He rocked forward and says, "One..." He rocked forward again, "Two..." then I felt all of his weight and we were falling out of the plane. My eyes got big. I barely felt the weight of the guide on my back having become adjusted to it. Falling at 120 mph, I started smiling. I didn't realize it at the time, but on the other side of fear there is a smile, a renewed sense of joy, that I was holding on to for dear life because I needed it to last. Then there was something in me that yearned to let go. I belched and my voice came out from the lower parts of my stomach and I screamed.

As I was falling through the sky, for the first time I truly felt free. The first time I felt as though fear no longer controlled me. I could conquer anything. I remembered a life of anxiety and doubt. Now, I could stand and tell the world that I had developed into a man with high self-esteem and integrity. I learned that fear is a temporary feeling that binds your head and your heart up when you are bound to do so much more. I could have been afraid and holding on for dear life, but I smiled instead. I made it this far, why not continue? I needed to get out there and try new things. Seeing the world from a different vantage point is healthier than not seeing it at all. From this small moment of falling 10,000 feet and counting, I saw houses, farmland, and buildings I might never walk into. There are so many things that seem to have such small detail until you get up close. I was falling for what seemed like forever. As I was screaming, I knew that this was what it truly felt like to be free and unbothered. This is how it felt to know success. This is what it was like to know and do exactly what you want to do and not let anybody or anything hinder you from doing it.

 I looked out over the horizon and knew that if God would have shown me my glory I would have ran away from it. I started looking at where I had been. I had to go through my teachers picking on me because of what they thought were my flaws. I had to look into the mirror and understand that my skin color recognizes my limitations, but my mindset can't and will not.

I had that uncomfortable feeling when your ear starts to pop and your heart is beating. You look out in the distance and you can see the skyline of the earth. The wind is blowing and the resistance is tough. Even if there is forward resistance in your progress, you can keep going, keep falling. The fall is much scarier than the results. I focused so much on how bad it could be instead of the opportunity that comes from it.

While I was still falling (at 120 mph). I began to have to rely on the person attached to me, he was supposed to pull the parachute. There were a multitude of people that were supposed give me a bad experience or a good one. It does not matter which side of the spectrum they fell on. They were put in place to help me with the weight that I needed to carry. I learned to listen to those people in my life that truly came into my life to help. They wanted to teach me something so they could make the weight of my responsibility easier to carry. For me, it was getting hit by a car and going through what seemed like hell. Being racially oppressed at such a young age, learning how to endure the pressure that someone else places on you—my past made me feel as though something was wrong with me. I learned however, that hard times don't last forever. Finding out that I was smart and a scholastic scholar, and that I could do anything I wanted to do, as long as I used my mind and my hands, or that smiling is contagious and it is the greatest universal language of all, were the things that allowed me to grow out of my past. I was able to deal with my lack of confidence and self-esteem from fear of not being accepted, and embrace who I was at my core and walk with my head high. Then there was my momma who practiced patience and prayer and my daddy who taught me discipline, manhood, and how to use my hands. Combined it gave me the ability to love, endure, and press through my situations to conquer them. The things I carried never got lighter, my strength to fly only became stronger.

Later on that year, I received news that I was going to be graduating from North Carolina A&T State University with a Bachelor's Degree in Information Technology—this would be my second degree. A few months later, I received some more news, I was offered to take on a job as a plant technology manager straight out of college—even after everyone said it wasn't possible. I went to church that Sunday and cried, thanking God for allowing me to be clay, so I could be molded even when it hurt. College and life experiences rushed over me and built me up to become so much more. I got up from my knees and wiped the tears from my eyes. I looked up and smiled and knew that this was not it for me. My goals were not here—they were above and beyond where I currently resided, but I was going to need help to get there. Every experience in life is a feather that strengthens your wings so you can soar. Why not use your experiences as feathers renew your strength and fly?

THE FEATHER OF MY WINGS

"But they who wait upon the LORD shall renew their strength; they shall mount up with wings as eagles, they run without growing weary, they walk without getting tired"

- Isaiah 40:31

THE FEATHER OF MY WINGS

Writing a book is an adventure. To begin with, it is a toy and an amusement. Then it becomes a mistress, then it becomes a master, then it becomes a tyrant. The Last phase is that just as you are about to be reconciled to your servitude, you kill the monster, and fling him to the public.

-Sir Winston Churchill

THE FEATHER OF MY WINGS

Connect With the Author

Website:

Httpps://www.jeromeljohn.com

Email:

Info.jeromeljohn@gmail.com

Twitter:

@jeromeljohn

Instagram:

@jeromeljohn

www.ingramcontent.com/pod-product-compliance
Lightning Source LLC
Chambersburg PA
CBHW051401290426
44108CB00015B/2111